AGAINST THE DEATH PENALTY

AGAINST THE DEATH PENALTY

CHRISTIAN AND SECULAR ARGUMENTS AGAINST CAPITAL PUNISHMENT

GARDNER C. HANKS

Herald
Press

Scottdale, Pennsylvania
Waterloo, Ontario

Library of Congress Cataloging-in-Publication Data
Hanks, Gardner C., 1947-
    Against the death penalty : Christian and secular arguments
against capital punishment / Gardner C. Hanks.
      p. cm.
    Includes bibliographical references and index.
    ISBN 0-8361-9075-0 (alk. paper)
    1. Capital punishment. 2. Capital punishment—Religious aspects—
Christianity. I. Title.
HV8694.H25 1997
364.66—dc21   97-18825

The paper used in this publication is recycled and meets the minimum requirements of American National Standard for Information Sciences—
Permanence of Paper for Printed Library Materials, ANSI Z39.48-1984.

AGAINST THE DEATH PENALTY
Copyright © 1997 by Herald Press, Scottdale, Pa. 15683
    Published simultaneously in Canada by Herald Press,
    Waterloo, Ont. N2L 6H7. All rights reserved
Library of Congress Catalog Number: 97-18825
International Standard Book Number: 0-8361-9075-0
Printed in the United States of America
Book and cover design by Paula M. Johnson

07 06 05 04 03 02 01 00 99 98 97 10 9 8 7 6 5 4 3 2 1

*In memory
of my mother,
Marion Chapman Hanks*

Contents

Foreword

Recently I heard a victim advocate say that although she has felt inclined against the death penalty, until now she has managed to put off the decision. Today the growing number of executions is forcing her into a corner where she feels she will have to take a stand.

For her, the issue is more pressing than for most of us. As a victim advocate in a state where executions are increasing, she likely will be asked to advise family members of murder victims and perhaps even witness executions with them.

Still, I suspect her situation is not unlike that of many of us: the growing momentum of executions is making it harder to avoid the issue. Thus in the past few months, the section on the death penalty in Mennonite Central Committee's web page on the Internet has been averaging one hundred "hits" or references per day. The popularity of the movie *Dead Man Walking*, which portrays the complexities and ambiguities of the issue, also shows that many are concerned.

Against the Death Penalty is for this victim advocate and for all those who have not decided where they stand on capital punishment. It is also for those who believe they are opposed to the death penalty and want further clarity on the issues and arguments.

Writer and churchman Will Campbell was once asked to represent the abolitionist perspective in a public debate on the death penalty. After supporters of the death penalty had made their arguments at length, it was Campbell's turn. On other occasions he had carefully presented the issues. But this time he simply walked to the podium and declared, "I'm opposed to the death penalty because it's just plain tacky." Then he sat down.

Although Campbell was right, Hanks' comprehensive but readable treatment is more helpful to most readers and shows more sensitivity for the feelings of murder victims' families. The book is exactly what the subtitle says: *Christian and Secular Arguments Against Capital Punishment.* One by one, Hanks addresses the issues, steering through them without becoming lost—no mean feat with a subject as complex and emotional as this one.

Ultimately, the issue is more fundamental than whether or not we favor the death penalty, and more basic than what form of punishment we will employ. Our concept of justice itself must be examined. Will we continue to pursue an approach to justice which leaves victims out, which focuses on establishing blame and administering pain while ignoring and even exacerbating wounds in the community? Or will we embrace a concept of justice that is more realistic and biblical, a justice that makes victims central while holding offenders accountable, a justice that seeks to heal and restore?

The death penalty debate is not about *whether* we draw lines between acceptable and unacceptable behavior but about *how* we do so. The way we answer that question depends on decisions which are even more basic: What do we expect of justice? In what kind of society do we wish to live?

The answer to these questions holds the key to our future.

—*Howard Zehr, Director of the Mennonite Central Committee US Office on Crime and Justice, Professor of Sociology and Restorative Justice at Eastern Mennonite University, and Author of* Changing Lenses: A New Focus for Crime and Justice, *and* Doing Life: Reflections of Men and Women Serving Life Sentences

Preface

This book has grown out of deep personal concern which is both religious and social. I have always been opposed to capital punishment. I was brought up in an abolitionist family and so acquired my opposition to the death penalty virtually at birth.

However, capital punishment was never a central issue for me until 1979. In the spring of that year, I became involved in the protests against the impending execution of John Spenkelink in Florida. Spenkelink was to be the first man executed against his will after a decade in which no executions had been carried out in the United States.

Spenkelink's execution and the weeks of demonstrations that preceded it were to have a profound impact on my life. The impending execution jolted me out of a political lethargy I had been in for several years. It also caused a sea change in my spiritual life.

The demonstrations against Spenkelink's execution had been organized by a large Presbyterian church in Tallahassee, Florida. The foresight of this church assured that people who opposed capital punishment had an organized way to express their feelings. In addition, it helped to guarantee that the demonstrations were founded on principles of nonviolence. Never before had I experienced this kind of church leadership on a social issue. I was impressed, and this led me to be less hostile to the faith this church represented.

Among the people who came to Florida to oppose the execution was a group of young Christian ministers from all over the South. These ministers quickly assumed a leadership role in the demonstrations. At critical times they moved demonstrators away from violence and back toward nonviolent protest. They probably saved a number of people from being hurt, perhaps even from being killed. As I increasingly looked to these men for leadership, I became more attracted to the faith from which they acted. One of these men frequently carried a sign that said, "We serve an executed Lord," a sentiment which served as the working title of this book.

Shortly after John Spenkelink was executed, my family and I moved away from Florida. Six months later, as an extension of the experience of seeing the Christian faith in action, I became a Christian. However, for the next nine years, I lived in two states —Iowa and Minnesota—which did not impose the death penalty. Because of that, capital punishment was not a central issue for me. I tried to put my faith into action in other peace-and-justice arenas.

In 1989, however, we moved to Idaho. At that time, Idaho had not executed anyone since 1957, but it did retain the death sentence. When I moved to the state, it had over twenty men on death row. And in 1994 Idaho did execute Keith Wells. Again I felt called to work on this issue.

As I looked around for groups that opposed the death penalty in Idaho, I found only two: Amnesty International and the American Civil Liberties Union. I was soon appointed as Amnesty International's State Death Penalty Action Coordinator. The small group of people from Amnesty International and the American Civil Liberties Union who were working actively on the death penalty were able to get legislation introduced in both 1991 and 1992 which would have excluded executions of mentally retarded defendants. Although we were not able to get the legislation out of committee, we took some consolation in getting a hearing for the bill in 1992. The sponsor for the bill that year was state senator Cynthia Scanlin, a minister from the United Church of Christ. The strongest support for the bill came from church organizations.

At the same time I was working on Idaho anti-death-penalty legislation, I became a spiritual adviser for a man on Idaho's death row. Our friendship began when he was considering giving up the appeals that were keeping him from being executed. In my Amnesty International role, I wrote and asked him to continue the appeals process. We then began to correspond, and he asked me to become his spiritual adviser.

I had never become so personally involved with an issue, but I decided this was something I was being called to do. Although there were times it was difficult, this friendship was one of the most rewarding of my life. I decided from the start that I would go as a friend and not as a proselytizer. However, after a few visits, he asked me if we could read the Bible together. Over the years we worked our way through most of the New Testament. Although we did not agree on many faith issues, our Bible reading was a rich experience for me. Our work together opened many new insights into Scripture which otherwise I would not have had.

Unfortunately, our relationship came to an end in 1993, when for reasons of his own, he decided he no longer wanted me to visit. Two years later another death row inmate asked me to become his spiritual adviser. I currently visit him several times a month.

My friendships with death row inmates and with family members of other men on death row have convinced me more than ever that the death penalty is opposed to everything the God I love and worship stands for. What once had been merely a matter of principle has now become an issue with human faces behind it. Because of that, I believe there will never be any turning back for me.

As I have worked on the issue of capital punishment over the past six years, I have often been frustrated by the lack of a concise information resource. There is much pertinent information, but it has often been published in pamphlets, survey tabulations, reports, and newspaper articles that would be difficult for most people to find. In addition, the information is scattered in many different sources and requires time and energy to compile. I have often wished for a reference source in which the various arguments against capital punishment were compiled along with pertinent facts, statistics, anecdotes, and quotes that supported those arguments.

In 1992 Cynthia Scanlin was defeated for reelection as part of an election that saw a much stronger pro-capital punishment majority elected in both houses of the Idaho legislature. It became apparent that there would not be much use in introducing anti-death penalty legislation again until the legislature changed. So I was left with time on my hands.

As the months went by, I increasingly felt the need to do something about the death penalty, but I wasn't sure what it was. Then I realized I had the time to put together the book of arguments against the death penalty that I had wanted. As a librarian, I had access to many sources of data, and I have also received much information over the years from Amnesty International, the American Civil Liberties Union, the National Coalition to Abolish the Death Penalty, and the Death Penalty Information Center. I decided that perhaps I was meant to write the book. My work of putting information together and the actual writing has confirmed this feeling.

As I have prepared the book, one issue has continually faced me. Who is the intended audience for the book? On one hand, my opposition to the death penalty is supported primarily by my Christian faith. Yet many people oppose the death penalty for secular reasons. I knew that if I approached the issue from a religious as well as from a social point of view, some secular readers might not use the material that would be applicable for them. After a great deal of thought and prayer, I decided the book must be true to its author. Although there is much information in the book that can be used to argue against the death penalty for secular reasons, the book begins and ends with religious reasons for opposing capital punishment.

In choosing to approach the subject matter this way, I have made the decision that the book will first address the Christian community. At the same time, however, it is my hope that secular death penalty opponents will also find the book useful. Certainly the information about biblical perspectives on the death penalty can be used when any death penalty abolitionist (whether religious or secular) addresses advocates of capital punishment who embrace the Judeo-Christian tradition.

I have also included a great deal of information about secular reasons for opposing capital punishment. Just before Idaho put Keith Wells to death, I wrote a guest opinion column for the local newspaper. I stated that while there was much research showing the death penalty to be ineffective, unfair, and detrimental to society, I was opposing it primarily for the moral reason that it is simply wrong to kill human beings. Shortly afterward, I received a letter asking me to prove that the death penalty did not prevent murders, that it had been applied to the innocent, and that it was expensive compared to life imprisonment. The letter stated that we could argue for a long time about the morality of capital punishment, but these facts would speak for themselves.

This letter showed me that for many people, secular arguments against capital punishment will be most effective. So I contend that Christian opponents of the death penalty should be acquainted with all reasons for opposing the death penalty, not just religious reasons. Therefore, a large part of this book addresses social issues to which people can relate, whether or not they share my faith.

The book is structured in the following manner. The first two chapters discuss the death penalty as addressed in the Old and New Testament. The next two chapters address the history of opposition to the death penalty in the West. Chapters five and six examine the deterrence theory regarding the death penalty—the idea that the death penalty keeps people from committing capital crimes—and provide a considerable amount of evidence that it does not. Chapter seven addresses the argument that the death penalty stops repeat offenders from carrying out further capital crimes. Chapter eight discusses the needs of the families of victims.

The next three chapters address injustices in applying the death penalty. Chapter nine examines the issues surrounding capital punishment and racial discrimination. Chapter ten looks at the mentally retarded, and chapter eleven focuses on defendants who are poor.

Chapter twelve shows that innocent people have been convicted of capital crimes and executed. Chapter thirteen looks at the tremendous fiscal costs of capital punishment.

Chapter fourteen examines the social costs. In chapter fifteen, we look at the death penalty as cruel and unusual punishment. Finally in chapter sixteen, we return to the realm of the spiritual and moral as the underlying basis for all arguments against the use of death as a punishment.

The chapters are followed by five appendixes. The first lists major court cases that have affected application of the death penalty since 1972. The next appendix gives statements of religious denominations in opposition to capital punishment. Another includes major statements by international organizations about the death penalty. One gives quotes by famous persons against capital punishment. The last appendix lists the names, addresses, and telephone numbers of organizations that are working against the death penalty in the United States.

I am aware that this book is not perfect and that much more information could have been included. I still hope the book will help those who oppose the death penalty to be able to debate the issue, using facts rather than sheer emotion.

I have found over the years that many people support the death penalty with little thought about what it really entails. Just hearing that other people do *not* support the death penalty will sometimes make proponents stop and think about their own position. The effect is even greater when we back up statements of opposition with credible information.

Let me offer a few comments on the book's style. I have tried to write rather informally. This is by no means an academic treatise, but I have included extensive notes. Citing credible sources of information can be a powerful addition to any debate on capital punishment, so I have given readers as many references as I could. I have tried to use inclusive language as much as possible. However, when writing of death row inmates, I have tended to use the male pronoun due to the fact that over 98 percent of inmates currently on death row are men.

I hope this book will be used in many ways. Letters to the editor, informal discussions, and formal presentations on the death penalty can all be enhanced by use of factual information. My greatest hope, however, is that this book will soon no longer be necessary. I pray that somehow Americans will come to their senses, as have the people of all other Western democracies, and that we will no longer feel that "killing people to show that killing people is wrong" makes any sense. On that day, I believe we will all be able to celebrate life as a gift that God has given to all people, a gift that neither the murderer nor the state has the right to take away.

—*Gardner C. Hanks*
  Boise, Idaho

Acknowledgments

No book is the work of one person working in a vacuum. That is particularly true of a book based on the research of many others. In the notes, the names of individual authors indicate the sources of my information. Many of the authors listed there have made major contributions to the intellectual arguments against the death penalty for many years. I know how lonely such opposition can be, and so these men and women have my greatest respect and gratitude.

A number of national death penalty abolitionist organizations have also provided information used in the book. These include the National Coalition to Abolish the Death Penalty, the Amnesty International Death Penalty Project, the Death Penalty Information Center, Murder Victims Families for Reconciliation, the NAACP Legal Defense and Educational Fund, and the American Civil Liberties Union. The information these organizations provide to capital punishment opponents is invaluable.

On a more personal note, I thank the small group of Idahoans who have worked with me for years against the death penalty in Idaho. These include Greg Jahn, George and Melva Patterson, Leo Griffard, Chris Schnoor, Bishop John Thornton, Dottie Blackwell, and Jack Van Valkenberg. They have often provided me with needed support. Bruce Bistline, who served as the Idaho ACLU lobbyist to the Idaho legislature in 1992, showed me the value of compiling information on the death penalty.

Over the years my congregation, the Hyde Park Mennonite Fellowship in Boise, Idaho, has given me support and been a sounding board for my ideas. They have also provided a financial subsidy for the book's publication. I am particularly thankful to Tim Cooper, my pastor, and to Larry Hauder, conference minister for Pacific Northwest Mennonite Conference, both of whom have encouraged me throughout the publication process.

My colleagues at the Idaho State Library have provided me with reference assistance. I particularly want to mention reference librarian Stephanie Kukay. She does not share my view of the death penalty, but in the finest tradition of our profession, she helped me find the information I needed. Our interlibrary loan assistant, Bill Church, has provided high-quality service. As a fellow writer, he offered enthusiastic encouragement. My fellow workers in the Library Development Division have probably heard more than they ever wanted to know about capital punishment and yet provided consistent and much-appreciated support.

Michael King at Herald Press was a most helpful and patient editor, and David Garber supervised the last stages of polishing the text. My friend Terri Wear helped create the index.

Last but certainly not least, I thank my family. My father and mother taught me the value of all human life. My original opposition to the death penalty came from them, along with the belief that if you see something wrong, you do something to fix it. My daughters Karin and Kathryn gave up many hours of their dad's time so this book could be written. Throughout the process, Suzie, my wife has been my greatest support. She diplomatically and correctly helped me edit the original manuscript. Without her help, this book would still be sitting in a cardboard cabinet next to the microwave.

AGAINST THE DEATH PENALTY

1
Life for Life? Old Testament Perspectives

The Bible is a source of values for many people in North America. The Old Testament is at the center of the Jewish faith and along with the New Testament speaks powerfully to all serious Christians.

Christians who defend capital punishment scripturally most often do so with references to the Old Testament. God told Noah after the flood, "Whoever sheds the blood of a human, by a human shall that person's blood be shed" (Gen. 9:6). This passage is frequently cited by death penalty advocates. These advocates also point to the many places in the Law where the death penalty is not only sanctioned but seemingly required.

It cannot be denied that certain Old Testament texts endorse capital punishment. Individual passages, however, need to be read in the context of the whole message of the Bible. When viewed in its entirety, the Old Testament is the story of a repeating cycle of redemption. God creates humans in his own image. Then comes human sin, God's forgiveness and reinstatement, human sin again, followed by God's forgiveness and reinstatement, and so on. This pattern, which mitigates against the final solution of the death penalty, begins with the fall of Adam and Eve and is seen clearly in the Genesis 4 story of the first murder.

The First Murder

Cain and Abel were two brothers, the sons of Adam and Eve. Cain became jealous of his brother when God looked more favorably on Abel's sacrifice than on Cain's. Cain lured his brother to an isolated place and then murdered him. In modern terminology, this was a first-degree murder: premeditated and cold-blooded. Cain then tried to cover up the murder, but the Lord uncovered the crime.

However, the Lord God did not take Cain's life for the murder. Instead, the punishment chosen was separation from the community by banishment. At the time the Bible was written, this was a severe punishment. Personal identity was so tied into community life that to be severed from the community was second only to death. Indeed, without the protection of the community, an individual was open to physical attack from anyone; one's life was put into real danger. As Cain put it, "I shall be a fugitive and a wanderer on the earth, and anyone who meets me may kill me."

However, God softened the punishment. He gave Cain protection. He declared that anyone who killed Cain would be required to suffer seven times the punishment given to Cain. God gave Cain a special mark to show this protection. Although Cain was punished severely, the story ends not with Cain's death, but with the birth of Cain's son Enoch. So God's answer to the murder of Abel was not death but a new life.

Noah and the Rule of Blood

How then do we move from the forgiveness and regeneration of Cain to the harsh words of God to Noah in Genesis 9:6? The text in question is part of God's blessing and instructions to Noah and his family after the Flood. Up until this time, human beings were not allowed to eat meat. Now, as the "golden age" of creation ended, God broke the harmony between humans and animals. Humans could now kill animals for food. However, there were limitations. The first was that humans could not eat the blood of animals, and the second was that they could not take human life, as they could an animal's life.

God told Noah that there would be a reckoning for killing other human beings. The text of Genesis 9:6 follows. "Whoever sheds the blood of a human, by a human shall that person's blood be shed." The passage certainly is descriptive of how life was at the time. The murder of a family member could bring the beginning of prolonged revenge-seeking in the form of a blood feud. Thus, a murder was not necessarily one isolated violent event; it could be one of many acts in a cycle of violence. In retaliation, one murder led to another murder, which led to another in further retaliation, and so on.

The sevenfold vengeance that God threatened for anyone who murdered Cain was the language of the blood feud. Thus Lamech claims in Genesis 4:23-24, "I have killed a man for wounding me, a young man for striking me. If Cain is avenged sevenfold, truly Lamech seventy-seven fold."

However, this raises a question. Is the text in Genesis 9:6 *prescriptive* or merely *descriptive*? Does this text tell us how God *wants* things to be or just how things are? In answering this question, the passage should not be taken out of context. The final line in the poetic text, a line rarely quoted by death penalty proponents, is important. "For in his own image God made humankind." The reason God does not want humans to kill each other is that in doing so, they destroy the very image of God. Nothing is said about a person losing this image-bearing characteristic when sin, even a murder, is committed. The killing of a murderer is as much the destruction of the image of God as is the killing of any other human being.

Moses the Murderer

One remarkable characteristic of the Old Testament narratives is the brutal honesty with which human nature is pictured. All human beings in the Old Testament are shown as deeply flawed. The stories abound with liars, cheaters, cowards, thieves, and murderers. Think of the three greatest human characters in the history of ancient Israel: Abraham nearly murdered his own son; Moses and David were both killers.

The story of the murder committed by Moses is told in Exodus 2:11-15. Moses, brought up in the royal household of an Egyptian princess, somehow discovered that he was actually a Hebrew. We can only imagine what he must have gone through psychologically at this point in his life. It must have been traumatic for him to find that he was not really a member of the Egyptian upper classes but instead a member of a clan of slaves. A modern equivalent might be for the son of a Fortune 500 family to discover he is really an adopted child from the ghetto.

To find out more about himself and his people, Moses went to visit the work camps where his relatives were laboring. During this visit, he began to identify with the slaves. When he saw one of the laborers being mistreated by an Egyptian overseer, he became incensed. But his response was calculated; he did not fly into a fit of rage and act on sheer impulse. The Bible tells us, "He looked this way and that, and seeing no one he killed the Egyptian and hid him in the sand" (Exod. 2:12).

Again, by modern standards this killing would probably be considered first-degree murder. The killing was calculated. Moses took some time to think about what he was going to do. If the victim was a government official, this would add to the severity of the crime, and it might even be looked on as an act of terrorism or revolt. Clearly the Egyptians saw the murder as a serious matter. The Bible tells us, "When Pharaoh heard of it, he sought to kill Moses" (Exod. 2:15).

At the time of the murder that Moses committed, the law given to Noah was still in force. Because the law was given to Noah, we must remember that it was universal—it applied to all human beings, not just to the Hebrews. Under Noachian law, to kill an Egyptian was as wrong as to kill a fellow Israelite.

In spite of this, God was merciful. Life for life was not required of Moses. God allowed him to escape the justice that the Egyptians would have imposed upon him. Like Cain, Moses was punished with exile. He was removed from all that he knew, from the protection of both his natural and his adoptive people. Yet God mitigated the punishment through his providential meeting with the daughters of Jethro, the priest of Midian. The rest of the story is well-known. Moses returned from exile to become the greatest leader the Israelites were ever to have, and one of the greatest lawgivers the world has ever known.

The Law

Given Moses' own history, it is ironic that Christian death penalty proponents find their strongest biblical support in the law he gave the Israelites. Capital punishment is a prominent part of the code of conduct contained in the Old Testament. The death penalty is invoked for many crimes, including murder (Exod. 21:12 et al.), rape of an engaged woman (Deut. 22:25), kidnapping (Exod. 21:16 et al.), adultery (Deut. 22:22), fornication by women (Deut. 22:20-21), incest (Lev. 20:11), male homosexuality (Lev. 20:13), having sex with animals (Exod. 22:19 et al.), idolatry (Deut. 17:2-5), sorcery (Lev. 20:27 et al.), false witness in a capital case (Deut. 19:18-19), prophecy in the name of other gods (Deut. 18:20), false prophecy (Deut. 18:20) cursing one's parents (Exod. 21:17), and rebelliousness on the part of a son (Deut. 21:18-21).

The Law in Its Time. For those of us who live in a more pluralistic, scientific, and less patriarchal society, the list seems excessive. Few of even the most adamant Jewish or Christian death penalty proponents would advocate the death penalty for all the offenses listed above. So this list must be viewed from a historical perspective if it is to teach us anything about how we should approach modern capital punishment.

First, we must recognize that capital punishment in the Old Testament was seen as a form of religious sacrifice. For a person to atone for a serious sin, that person's life must be forfeit. Much as sacrificing an animal paid God back for less-serious crimes, human sacrifice through the death penalty restored the balance of justice after a more serious crime had been committed. This belief, deeply embedded in human consciousness, predated the Mosaic law and can still be heard in arguments for the death penalty today. For example, the idea that the death penalty must exist to "balance out" murder or "to make things right" is a secular expression of this belief.

Before the law existed, families were responsible for seeking the human sacrifice that would atone for a serious crime committed against one of its members. This system led to an unregulated cycle of violence, in which families could be trapped into continuous and deadly conflict with each other. When such a blood feud arose, every member of both families, no matter how innocent of any crime, was subject to deadly attacks.

Old Testament scholars have long recognized that the Mosaic law was meant to be a limitation on violence rather than an endorsement of it.[1] The written laws came into Israel's history at a time when the community was passing from a nomadic, tribal society to a more stable, agricultural society with a more centralized government. Although the law contains elements of both the older and the newer ways of approaching social conflicts, in general it reflects a movement away from the blood feud and negotiation between families as a method of social control to a more "bureaucratic" approach to justice, with priests or village elders acting as judges.

One important passage that clearly reflects this change is Deuteronomy 24:16. "Parents shall not be put to death for their children, nor shall children be put to death for their parents; only for their own crimes may persons be put to death." In these brief words, the law eliminates the blood feud as a socially acceptable method of seeking justice. Families are no longer allowed to retaliate against a murderer's family. The law demands that only the actual offender be punished.

Thus while the law may appear to be excessively violent by modern standards, it actually was intended to reduce the level of violence. When Exodus 21:23-24 says, "Life for a life, eye for eye, tooth for tooth," the law actually means, "No more than a life for a life; no more than an eye for an eye; no more than a tooth for a tooth." Before the law, clans could choose to seek revenge at whatever level they wished. The only limitation was the possible retaliation of the other family. Large, powerful clans were at an obvious advantage under this system. The law was a great equalizer in this regard.

The law made justice less dependent on personal whims and social power. The message behind the law was that God is working through the community and will provide both victims and offenders with justice. Relatives of a victim who has been murdered, raped, or maimed are too emotionally involved to rationally decide what is best for the community. While revenge may make the victim or the victim's family feel better in the short run, the long-term effects of such decisions may be disastrous for the community as a whole. The law put a definite limit on the allowable retaliation for a crime. At the same time it provided victims with justice.

This is seen in the one text of the Old Testament that most clearly mandates the death penalty, Numbers 35:30-34. The passage calls for the death penalty for a murderer and does not. allow ransom in place of it. Ransom, of course, would be more possible for the rich and powerful family than for the poor. This text then puts the rich murderer and the poor murderer on the same level. The rich person cannot murder the poor person with impunity, because the penalty is death. Here God is telling us that a life is a life. Money cannot bring a human life into the world and so it should not be possible for money to purchase the right to take a human life. Under the law the lives of all people in the community are equal, with the exception of slaves (see Exod. 21:20).

Witness Requirements. If nothing else, the law slowed down the process of revenge. Unlike the blood feud, where retaliation could be carried out whenever and however the offended party wished, the law required that there be a process at which witnesses would bring forth testimony about what had occurred. In the Deuteronomic code, there were three important provisions about these witnesses.

The first provision was that there must be more than one witness in order for a person to be convicted. Deuteronomy 19:15 stipulates, "A single witness shall not suffice to convict a person of any crime or wrongdoing in connection with any offense that may be committed. Only on the evidence of two or three witnesses shall a charge be sustained." Numbers 35:30 mentions this requirement particularly with regard to capital cases: "No one shall be put to death on the testimony of a single witness."

Given that the methods of modern criminology were not available and that cases were handled with dispatch, it can be assumed that "witnesses" in the Deuteronomic code refers primarily to eyewitnesses. It is a high standard to require this degree of proof, having at least two eyewitnesses. Murder is frequently committed in secret. When other people are present at a murder, they are often involved in one way or another—thus making them suspect as witnesses.

The second Deuteronomic rule regarding witnesses was that they must also act as the executioners in capital cases. Unlike modern society, which holds its executions in private, Old Testament society held public executions. Those who provided the testimony to bring about a death sentence were expected to help carry it out. "The hands of the witnesses shall be the first raised against the person to execute the death penalty . . ." (Deut. 17:7). For witnesses in the Old Testament, there was nothing isolated about the process of testifying in a capital case. They would help carry out the execution that resulted from their testimony. The words that the witness used had immediate and bloody impacts that the witness could not escape. Such a provision would obviously discourage people from testifying.

The final Deuteronomic provision for witnesses regarded the penalty for false testimony and followed the ninth commandment: "You shall not bear false witness against your neighbor" (Exod. 20:16; Deut. 5:20). Deuteronomy 19:18-19 states, "If the witness is a false witness, having testified falsely against another, then you shall do to the false witness just as the false witness had meant to do to the other." Under this law the penalty for perjury in a capital case would be the death penalty. Witnesses were required to be answerable for what they said. The serious implications of bearing false witness would make witnesses careful to tell the truth as clearly and as simply as possible, without embellishments or inferences.

With these provisions for witnessing, the Mosaic law was intended to be as fair as possible to the accused person. Given human nature, these laws were undoubtedly disregarded at times, but the law as a whole stressed that it should not be easy to convict someone of a crime, especially when the penalty was death. Indeed, if the standards for testimony used in the Deuteronomic law were applied in our own criminal justice system, it is doubtful that there would be many convictions in death penalty cases.

The Cities of Refuge. To the above provisions, the law also added a unique system for the further protection of the unintentional killer. The system is described in Numbers 35:22-28 and Deuteronomy 19:4-13. For unintentional homicides, the law set up a number of cities of refuge. If the killer could escape to the city, and if the congregation found that the homicide was unintentional, he could remain in the city of refuge in safety. The avenger of blood (a holdover concept from the blood feud in which the victim's next of kin acted as executioner) could not take revenge on him. However, if the congregation found that the murder was intentional, or if the murderer left the city of refuge before the death of the high priest, then the avenger could kill him.

As with the requirements for witnesses, the cities of refuge limited the revenge that could be taken for a homicide. The law of the cities of refuge recognized that there could be degrees of culpability in homicide. A homicide that was unintentional, what in modern terms would be called "manslaughter," was recognized as different from the intentional killing of another human being. Under the rule of the blood feud, making such a distinction was strictly up to the clans involved. In God's law, however, a study of the intent of the killer was required. And as a result, the level of potential violence was lessened.

The Death Penalty in the Life of the Community

In large measure, the Old Testament is a national religious history of Israel and Judah. As a result, we gain relatively little insight into the daily life of the common people. The few executions that are reported in the Old Testament, such as the stoning of Achan in Joshua 7 and the killing of Shimei in 1 Kings 2, are religious or political in nature.

In spite of this, we know that the death penalty was in use from two capital cases described in the New Testament—the near stoning of the woman caught in adultery (John 8:1-11), and the stoning of Stephen for blasphemy (Acts 6 and 7). Although we will discuss these stories more thoroughly in the next chapter, it is clear that both describe authentically the way executions would be carried out.

However, were executions common in Old Testament times? There is little evidence in the Bible. Over time scribal and rabbinic interpretations of the law influenced Judaism against the use of the death penalty. By the second century B.C., executions were rarely carried out by Jewish authorities.[2] Cross-examination of prosecution witnesses was rigorous, as in the second century B.C. book of Susanna, in the Apocrypha. But cross-examination of defense witnesses was strictly controlled. Judges were required to fast a full day before rendering a verdict. Even up to the point of the actual execution, defendants were given the chance to provide mitigating evidence.

On the way to the execution, a herald announced the name of the condemned and the witnesses against him, and asked for others to come forward to show that the execution was unwarranted. The condemned was allowed to stop four times to offer further arguments against the execution himself. Under these conditions, executions rarely occurred. The Talmud tells of one Sanhedrin that approved of only one execution in a seventy-year period.[3] In the first two centuries of this common era, the rabbis called for careful trial procedures, as shown in the tractate Sanhedrin in the Mishnah.

In smaller communities, conflicts probably continued to be worked out informally. Most of the people of Israel lived in small, preindustrial, agricultural villages. In such communities, social interaction among community members would have been high. While the use of the blood feud would have become more limited in settled communities, negotiated settlements of disputes were undoubtedly used extensively. For example, when Joseph found that Mary was pregnant, which implied that she had committed the capital crime of fornication, he simply decided to "dismiss her quietly" (Matt. 1:19; Deut. 22:20-21). This, it would seem, was the typical way under Mosaic law of dealing with many capital crimes.

David the Murderer

While the bureaucratization of justice under the law to some extent equalized the position of the common people, there were some whom the law would barely touch. These were people who became the royalty and the aristocrats of the new nation. In this context, we approach the story of David's murder of Uriah and its consequences, as told in 2 Samuel 11 and 12.

David was king of Israel, living in Jerusalem. Over the years he had been able to gather a loyal group of followers, and his position was strong enough that he no longer had to go to war himself. One day, as his army was in the field, he was strolling on the roof of the king's house and noticed a beautiful woman bathing nearby, likely in the presumed seclusion of a neighboring garden. David yielded to lust. Despite the fact that the woman was the wife of Uriah, one of his most loyal soldiers, he seduced her.

When she became pregnant, he recognized that he had a serious problem. The loyalty of his troops depended to some extent on his moral leadership. Because of this, David called Uriah home from the war in hopes that Uriah would have sex with his wife, then think the baby his own. But Uriah was too loyal. He refused to sleep with his wife as long as his comrades were still in battle.

Finally David sent Uriah back to the war but also sent instructions to his commander Joab to make sure Uriah was killed in battle. Uriah was placed at the center of the action, then other troops were withdrawn from around him. Uriah was killed.

God recognized what had happened, however, and sent the prophet Nathan to accuse David of the crime. According to the law, David had committed two capital offenses: adultery and deliberate murder. As king, however, David was too powerful to be subject to the human administration of the law. He was not tried for adultery and murder, although what had happened must have been obvious to many around him, even before it was announced publicly by Nathan. From a human viewpoint, the law broke down when powerful people could avoid its condemnation. Only God could punish the king.

In David's sin and its consequences, weaknesses of the law became apparent. Such weaknesses were reaffirmed in the subsequent histories of both Judah and Israel. While the law itself may have been intended to equalize the position of community members, in reality the human administration of the law continued to treat people differently. The rich and the powerful could still "get away with murder." It was this weakness that called for an entirely new social arrangement—a new society of God's reign shown in the New Testament.

Applications of Old Testament Principles to Our Situation

Before we see what the New Testament has to say about the death penalty, however, we will summarize some of the important lessons about capital punishment found in the Old Testament. We will measure what they might have to say about the current use of the death penalty in the United States.

Punishment Must Be Applied Justly. The first lesson is that God intends for us to move away from arbitrary and capricious retaliation into a more systematic approach to justice. The death penalty as applied in the United States in the late twentieth century, however, is used arbitrarily and capriciously.[4] Whether a person receives the death penalty depends on a number of factors, most of which have nothing to do with the severity of the crime. For example, geography plays an important factor. In twelve states and the District of Columbia, there is no capital punishment, so murders committed there will not result in the death penalty. On the other hand, murderers in the Deep South are more likely to receive the death penalty than in other parts of the country.[5]

In some states, murders committed in one county are more likely to result in a death sentence than murders committed in other counties. A recent case in Idaho, for instance, was resolved when a small, poor, rural county chose to no longer pursue the death penalty after it had spent more than $400,000 on the case. The same case brought in a richer county, however, would continue to be prosecuted.

Another arbitrary factor in death penalty sentencing is

race. While only 12 percent of the population is African-American, 40 percent of the people on death row are black.[6] Another group overrepresented on death row are the mentally retarded. While the retarded make up only 3 percent of the general population, it is estimated that about 10 percent of death row inmates are mentally retarded.[7]

The one characteristic of almost all people who receive the death penalty, however, is that they are poor. In 1988, of the 226 people on California's death row, only two had enough money to hire their own attorney for appeals.[8] Unlike the Old Testament imperative that all murder defendants be treated the same, regardless of their ability to pay for ransom, rich defendants in the United States will probably be able to "ransom" themselves off death row by hiring their own lawyer, whereas the poor defendant will have to depend on overworked and often inexperienced public defenders.

These factors have combined to make the application of capital punishment so arbitrary that in 1997 the American Bar Association called for a moritorium on executions until the system could insure greater fairness. Even the lawyers who administer the system do not believe it provides adequate safeguards against injustice.

With these issues in mind, it is obvious that capital punishment, as applied in the United States, does not meet the Old Testament requirement that it be applied in a fair and equitable manner.

All Victims Have Equal Value. Closely related to this idea of the fair application of the death sentence for offenders is that all victims should also be equal in the eyes of the law. The blood feud was unfair because it allowed more powerful families to retaliate with impunity for its victimized members. Less powerful families were less able to seek equal revenge.

In our society, the death penalty is more often imposed on killers who murder white people than on those who murder African-Americans. Cases involving white murder victims more often draw death penalties than cases involving African-American victims. This shows that the criminal justice system does not treat victims equally.[9]

The use of victim impact statements should also be an important issue in this regard. Victims or victim families that can make a "good appearance" in court will more likely be able to bring about a death sentence than the victims or victim families who do not appear to be as "valuable." Under this system, the murderer of a wealthy person will more likely receive a death penalty than the murderer of a poor person, especially if the victim appears to be "undesirable" in the eyes of white, upper middle-class judges and prosecutors.

It is important that families of victims be allowed to tell their story. But when they do this in an adversarial setting, it can create injustice and further victimization.

Levels of Culpability. The concept of the cities of refuge recognized that there could be different levels of culpability in homicides. In present-day United States, however, we are moving away from such distinctions. The mentally retarded are over-represented on our nation's death row. This indicates that we do not recognize the defendant's level of ability to understand the crime as an important factor when deciding on a sentence. In fact, because mentally retarded people are regarded by many as less beneficial to society, it appears that mental retardation is regarded as an aggravating rather than mitigating factor in capital murder cases.

In addition, under current court rulings, mental illness is regarded as less a mitigating factor in a capital case than it has been in the past. Some states have even disallowed mental illness as a recent defense in a criminal case.

Even age is more likely to be disregarded than it was in the recent past, with defendants as young as sixteen now receiving the death penalty. The historic trend away from punishing children and youth with death appears to be stalled or even turned around.

The Importance of Proper Judicial Procedures. The Old Testament set out a series of important considerations for witnesses. Such procedures made it more difficult to sentence a defendant to death. The current U.S. Supreme Court, however, does not require that all the judicial rules be followed. The doctrine of "harmless error" makes it easier for the prosecutor to bend or even break the law in trying a capital case. While the Supreme Court holds that the defendant must obey the law, it does not require the government to do so.[10] This is distant from the principles set forth in the Old Testament.

Impartial Judges. The strong emphasis on the importance of witnesses in the Old Testament implies that judgment is to be made on the facts of the case at hand, not on a general feeling about the defendant or the politics of the situation.

In our society, however, final decisions on capital cases are usually made by judges and other government officials, many of whom have had to show that they are "tough" on crime in order to get appointed or elected to their position. In the words of Howard Zehr, "In the past two decades, governors have become increasingly unwilling to take political risks by granting clemency. Commutations of death or even life sentences are rare events in most states. For example, only two death row prisoners were granted clemency in 1992."[11] There were over 2600 men and women on U.S. death rows in 1992.

Conclusion

While the Old Testament does not forbid the death penalty, it imposes stringent criteria for its use. The Old Testament is concerned for justice and belief in a God who ultimately prefers to restore rather than to punish. This worked against widespread executions.

In addition, one of the great lessons of the Old Testament is that all nations, all social systems, even those special in God's eyes, fail to live up to his standards. True justice will not be found in any system that depends on human administration. People who are rich and powerful will always be treated better within the criminal justice system than those who are poor and weak. With this realization, we now turn to God's powerful new covenant made through the life and execution of the Son of man, the quintessential representative of the poor and the weak—those who suffer most at the hands of human justice systems.

2
One Without Sin: New Testament Perspectives

Whereas the Old Testament allowed the death penalty under certain stringent conditions, the New Testament closed off the possibility of any support for capital punishment. In the New Testament, Jesus creates the kingdom of God, a new social order not dependent on the use of political, social, or police power. Under this new social arrangement, love—not violence —is paramount. Since killing and revenge are incompatible with love, it should be obvious that capital punishment cannot be part of the reign of God inaugurated through Jesus Christ.

Jesus Stops an Execution

There can be no question about Jesus' attitude toward the death penalty. He did not deal with some controversial issues. But in the story of John 8:1-11, he did speak about capital punishment. Jesus was teaching in the temple when the scribes and Pharisees approached him with a woman caught in the act of adultery. According to the law, adultery was a capital offense (Deut. 22:22). Apparently they were not too concerned about evenhanded justice since they did not also bring the man who committed adultery with this woman.

Jesus realized that their purpose for bringing the problem to him was to trap him into saying something inappropriate and blasphemous. So he didn't hurry his answer. Finally he told them, "Let anyone among you who is without sin be the first to throw a stone at her."

The merciful reasonableness of Jesus' approach to the

problem diluted the blood lust of the crowd. They were forced to think about what they were doing. Ashamed of themselves, they slipped away. Jesus then told the woman that he, too, did not condemn her. "Go, . . . and do not sin again."

The approach that Jesus took to capital crime was in accordance with his approach to sin, forgiveness, and redemption in general. For Jesus, sin was sin; there was no sin worse than any other. All sin represented the human desire to control others, to make others into objects that exist only for our own benefit. Sin is our unholy desire "to be like God" (Gen. 3:5; Ezek. 28:2) in the sense that it is the human obsession to be in charge, to be at the center of the universe.

According to Jesus, this sinfulness could come out in acts or words or even thoughts. In the Sermon on the Mount (Matt. 5:21-30), he equates murder with verbal insults and anger. In the same way, for Jesus there was no difference between actually committing adultery and harboring lustful thoughts. In either case, we belittle the importance of another human being.

In this sense, the law that Jesus gave us was a more stringent law than the Mosaic law of the Old Testament. But the answer Jesus made to all sin, whether that sin came out in the form of an angry word or a murder, was a merciful forgiveness that challenged the mind-set of violence and vengeance. "Love your enemies and pray for those who persecute you," Jesus told his followers (Matt. 5:44).

Thus the response Jesus gave to the crowd who wanted to execute the adulteress was simply a logical extension of his approach to sinfulness in general. We have the right to kill only when we ourselves are blameless. Since we are never blameless, we never have the right to kill. Instead, our reaction to sin must be forgiveness, even as we ask for the forgiveness of our own sins. If we cannot forgive others, then we have no right to expect anyone, including God, to forgive our sins. Jesus made this explicit in Matthew 6:14-15. "For if you forgive others their trespasses, your heavenly Father will also forgive you; but if you do not forgive others, neither will your Father forgive your trespasses."

The Most Famous Execution

That Christians should oppose the death penalty is clear in what Jesus taught during his ministry, and it can also be found in the example set by his own death. When Christians are tempted to think that support for capital punishment is compatible with their faith, they should consider carefully that they serve a Lord who himself was the victim of the death penalty.

The Hollywood portrayals of the death of Jesus have made us think of it in terms of heroes and villains. Jesus is seen as the hero; Caiaphas, Pilate, and Herod are shown as villains. Caiaphas is a scheming and power-mad politician. Pilate is a weak and vacillating judge. Herod is the mad king more interested in Jesus' ability to perform miracles than in the facts of his criminal case.

Such portrayals may lead us to believe that Jesus' trial was held in an uncivilized society, and that his death may have been avoided if a more reasonable and less capricious legal system had been in place. We may come out of such movies, for example, wishing that Jesus had been tried under the American judicial system—that *our* system could never have committed such a blatant injustice.

The facts, however, are quite different. Jesus Christ was tried in the most moral country of his time. He was tried under a system of justice that, while harsh, was systematic and strove to be fair. This fact has much to teach us about the fallibility of human morality and justice, even at their best.

Jewish Morality. Throughout the Roman Empire, the Jewish population was known as one of the most moral elements of society. Many people who sought a more moral way of life attended synagogue services and accepted all but the most ritualistic aspects of Jewish law. These groups of God seekers, God fearers, or proselytes were to become one of the most important sources of members for the early Christian church (Acts 2:10, 10:2; 13:43).

The moral value of the Jewish population to the Roman Empire was recognized by exempting Jews from certain religious obligations they could not follow under Jewish law. These laws and the moral separateness of the Jews also at times led to resentment which could boil up into vicious pogroms and other measures against them. As with all moral people, the Jewish population was viewed with a mixture of respect, distrust, guilt, and hatred.

The headquarters of the Jewish religion was the temple at Jerusalem. The great religious teachers lived and worked in the city where Christ was tried. Students of the law, such as the young Saul (Paul), traveled to Jerusalem to learn from these great masters. The Sanhedrin, the Jewish legislative body that tried Jesus, included some of these teachers of the law as well as the political leaders of the Jewish people in Judea.

Because the trial was also held at the time of Passover, we surmise that the Jewish leaders would have been especially careful to follow the law to the greatest degree possible. Violations of the law could have led to serious rioting, as the leaders recognized in Matthew 26:5.

The reports of the trial in Matthew 26:57-68 and Mark 14:53-65, however, do seem to contain deviations from rules for sessions of the Sanhedrin. The meeting was not held at the prescribed place; the meeting was held at night; the verdict was not postponed by a day; and the rules of evidence were abused. The account in Luke 22:66 tells a different story of a daytime trial. Experts have suggested that the meeting reported in Matthew and Mark may have been a pretrial hearing and that Luke reports the true trial.[1]

Whatever happened, the Bible does not tell of an uproar because of a serious violation of the law, something that would surely have occurred if zealous teachers of the law had been aware of such violations. Perhaps there are two explanations for this. Either the laws were not broken, or the violations were held to be minor—"harmless error," to use the term the United States Supreme Court applies to minor judicial infractions in modern criminal cases.

This latter possibility may have occurred because the Sanhedrin did not have the power to condemn a man to death; only the Romans could do that. Under these circumstances, perhaps the leaders were willing to follow informal procedures. Indeed, they may have even felt that their proceedings or "trial" under

Jewish law had little meaning when a person could only be condemned in the administration of Roman law. In either case it seems clear that the chief Jewish leaders felt that Jesus had received a fair hearing that did not violate the law in any substantial way.

Roman Justice. But what then of the Roman law? Although the Roman legal system could be harsh, its principles were based on a desire for fairness, especially for Roman citizens. Paul's appeals for justice based on his Roman citizenship in Acts 16:37-39; 22:23-29; and 25:9-12 indicate the power that citizens held under the law. Principles of Roman law have influenced legal systems from that time forward. In fact, some principles of Roman law are still found in American jurisprudence. In short, the Roman system of justice was one of history's great legal systems.

The Pilate pictured in the Bible was hardly an example of Roman virtue. Yet, it is also obvious that he felt he needed a better reason than first given by the Jewish leaders to execute Jesus. When the trial opened, he found that Jesus was not in violation of any Roman law. Although he was willing to have him flogged to appease the Jewish leadership, he found no cause to condemn Jesus to death (Luke 23:13-23).

Pilate was finally convinced to crucify Jesus for reasons more political than legal. As the Roman governor, he had to deal with "messiahs" on a fairly regular basis. He undoubtedly recognized the political as well as religious meaning of that term. While Jesus had done nothing that warranted the death penalty, the claims being made about him made him dangerous. Caiaphas and his followers recognized that Pilate would have to act if Jesus was seen as a real danger to Roman rule. Thus, in bringing the case to Pilate, their charges of blasphemy were much less important than their view of Jesus' potential political position.

The most important accusation they made was this: "We found this man perverting our nation, forbidding us to pay taxes to the emperor, and saying that he himself is the Messiah, a king" (Luke 23:2). If Jesus was a threat to the empire, Pilate had no choice but to execute him. Pilate was still not fully convinced, however. But the political threat was demonstrated by the potential riot that was brewing and the crowd's questioning of his own loyalty to the emperor. Thus, Pilate finally chose to condemn Jesus as "King of the Jews" (John 19:19; Mark 15:18).

The execution of Jesus, then, demonstrates the flawed nature of all human systems of morality and law. When principles come into conflict with perceived practical needs, principles are often laid aside. Justice is almost always a casualty of political necessity. The death of Jesus on the cross strips off the veneer of respectability that covers the powers and principalities that control the social, political, and legal systems of our fallen world (Col. 2:14-15). Jesus' death should not lead to the condemnation of the Jewish leaders (much less the Jewish people) or the Roman leadership. Instead, it points to the injustice that contaminates *all* nations and their systems of justice.

The Crucifixion as the Final Sacrifice. In Christian theology, Jesus' death on the cross is much more than an example of human injustice. Jesus' death is in some mysterious way redemptive. In the Old Testament, animal sacrifice and capital punishment were meant to atone for individual sins, thereby reestablishing the moral balance that sin destroyed. According to the New Testament, Christ's death atoned for all human sin: past, present, and future. First John 2:2 states, "He is the atoning sacrifice for our sins, and not for ours only but also for the sins of the whole world" (see also Rom. 5:22-26; 2 Cor. 5:17, 21; Heb. 10:10, 14; 1 John 4:7-12).

Jesus' death removed the need for the animal sacrifices required in the Old Testament; his death was the final and all-redeeming sacrifice. Similarly, his death also removed the need for the human sacrifice of capital punishment. Because Jesus has righted the moral balance for all time, we no longer have to make sacrifices, either animal or human, to make things right. This is what frees his disciples to forgive those who have broken the moral order.

To support the death penalty, then, is to bring into question the efficacy of Christ's sacrifice. God loves all people, no matter what they have done. As Paul puts it in Romans 5:6-10,

While we were still weak, at the right time Christ died for the un-
godly. .... While we still were sinners Christ died for us. ....
While we were enemies, we were reconciled to God through the
death of his Son.

To place limits on Christ's redemptive act on the cross
strikes at the very heart of Christian theology. If the death of
Christ did not answer for all sinners, then how can we be sure
that Christ died for *our* sins? If Christ's death is not for all, it is
merely another in a long line of martyrs' deaths and as such can
have no special theological significance. But if Christ died for all
men and women, then we cannot limit the meaning of the cross
even for the worst murderer. The sin of the murderer is an-
swered by the cross of Christ. There is no further requirement
for punishment. We should not destroy those for whom Christ
died (1 Cor. 8:11).

Society may still protect itself by separating the dangerous
criminal from other people. Yet from a Christian point of view,
this should be done as a redemptive act, not as a punitive one.
The death penalty which has no redemptive purpose, then,
must not be used.

Other New Testament Executions

Although the execution of Jesus has the most to teach us
about the death penalty, there are other executions in the New
Testament. Each has something unique to say about capital
punishment.

John the Baptist. The execution of John the Baptist shows
how the death penalty can be used by tyrants in a completely
arbitrary and casual way. The story is found in Matthew 14:1-9
and Mark 6:17-29. John the Baptist was thrown in prison at the
insistence of Herodias, the wife of King Herod. Herodias hated
John because he had questioned the legality of her marriage to
Herod, raising both moral and political implications. Although
Herod himself was not inclined to have John executed, Herodias wanted to see him killed. She was able to get her way by
manipulating Herod when he was hosting a party.

After Herodias's daughter performed a dance, Herod

promised to give the girl anything she wanted. Herodias told her daughter to ask for John's execution. Herod then was put into the embarrassing position of either breaking his oath or killing a man he did not want to kill. Herod chose to have John executed, possibly because breaking his oath could have weakened his political prestige.

The story illustrates one of the real dangers of the death penalty. It can be used by an unscrupulous leader to do away with opponents and prophetic critics. The death penalty has been used in this way throughout history. Under a tyrant, the death penalty allows that despot to permanently eliminate opponents in a manner that is perfectly legal. As will be shown in chapter fourteen, even in democracies the death penalty has at times been used to silence unpopular political figures.

The Two Thieves. Because the death of Jesus is the focus of Good Friday, we sometimes forget that two other men were executed that day. The story of these two men as it is told in Luke 23:32-43 points to another important New Testament teaching about the death penalty. Jesus was crucified between the two criminals. One of the criminals joined the rest of the crowd in deriding the Savior, but the second told the first thief,

> "Do you not fear God, since you are under the same sentence of condemnation? And we indeed have been condemned justly, for we are getting what we deserve for our deeds, but this man has done nothing wrong." Then he said, "Jesus, remember me when you come into your kingdom." Jesus then accepted him and told him, "Truly I tell you, today you will be with me in Paradise."

The message of the execution of the good thief is an important one for Christians. The history of redemption for each individual is unique. For some it will come early. For others it may come only at the last minute. Christians, then, cannot give up on anyone. Even the worst criminal, like the good thief, may repent. Like Jesus himself, Christians must always be prepared to receive the repentant sinner.

Those who use capital punishment, however, assume that there are some people so evil that they cannot be redeemed. They also assume that society can know which people are redeemable and which people are not. The last-minute conversion of the good thief refutes these assumptions.

Stephen. The last execution described in detail in the New Testament is the martyrdom of Stephen, one of the original deacons of the Jerusalem church. The story can be found in Acts 6 and 7. Stephen was a powerful speaker. His abilities made him a leader in the early church and a successful evangelist. For these very reasons, Stephen was considered dangerous.

Because the early church was an unpopular minority in Jerusalem, and because Stephen was a symbolic leader of the Christian movement, it was easy for his enemies to have him summarily tried and executed. He was arrested and brought before the council. False witnesses were produced against him. Then Stephen spoke, but his words only inflamed a crowd that had already condemned him. So he was rushed from the council chambers and executed, with no chance of appeal.

This kind of legal "lynching" may not be prominent in the United States at the moment, but at times it has been. In the past, executions of African-Americans in the South were often held after only cursory trials, with the result a foregone conclusion. The current trend of court rulings that will speed up the execution process and limit the right of appeals may once again open up the possibility of this kind of trial and execution.

James. The execution of James is briefly described in Acts 12:2. James was executed by Herod, primarily to solidify Herod's position with the Jewish leadership. The execution was held for political reasons. Such executions are not uncommon in America. Politicians have long recognized that the death penalty is popular with the American public. Many have cynically supported it, even when it does not fit into the rest of their political agenda.

During the 1992 political campaign, Bill Clinton went to Arkansas to oversee the execution of Rickey Ray Rector. Rector was so brain damaged he spent much of his time howling. If it had not been an election year, and if Clinton had not been in the midst of a campaign in which he had to show himself tough on crime, perhaps he could have offered more mercy. However, mercy at that time in his campaign would have been political suicide. Clinton chose the politically expedient course. Rickey Ray Rector died.[2] Sadly, the use of executions for this kind of political purpose is not uncommon in our country.

The Authorities and the Sword

There are an overwhelming number of scriptural passages against the death penalty in the Gospels. For this reason, Christian death penalty proponents rarely appeal to the Gospels to support their belief. The one New Testament passage to which they may appeal is Romans 13:3-4.

> For rulers are not a terror to good conduct, but to bad. Do you wish to have no fear of the authority? Then do what is good, and you will receive its approval; for it is God's servant for your good. But if you do what is wrong, you should be afraid, for the authority does not bear the sword in vain! It is the servant of God to execute wrath on the wrongdoer.

This passage appears to lend some support for capital punishment. This is true, however, only if the text is read out of context. The word that has been translated "sword" in this passage is *machaira*, a symbol of authority but not the weapon used by the Romans in carrying out executions.[3]

The early Christian church was a revolutionary movement. Some of the epistles—both of Paul and of other writers—show that, like most revolutionary movements, the church was attracting people who felt that the new social order gave them the right to do whatever they liked. Their behavior endangered the position of the church. Paul warned the churches that, to the degree it was possible without violating the law of God, Christians should obey the government.

For Paul, the state was a necessary structure in a fallen world. Through its police power, it kept a semblance of peace and therefore had the right to use reasonable force to carry out this function. Paul's observations about the role of government in Romans 13, quoted above, reflect this view.

At the time Paul was writing, however, Christians could not participate in government as officials, because they would not take the oath of allegiance to the emperor. They believed that such an oath of allegiance would have run counter to their allegiance to Jesus as Lord.

Romans 13 was written to a group of people who were not participants in government. They were people who had to live under the authority of a government over which they had no control. Given this situation, Paul suggested that they adopt a nonprovocative attitude toward the state. Even though Christians were not answerable to the government in the same way they were to their Lord, they still needed to respect its purpose as given by God.

This did not mean Christians had to approve of everything the government did. The martyrdoms of the disciples and of Paul himself show that the first Christians did not give the authorities unlimited approval. Paul, however, was also a realist. He recognized that the state sometimes would use force to carry out its function of restraining evil. At the same time, Paul saw that governmental control was only a temporary and partial solution to evil. Christ's way was more perfect—the way of love, as described in Romans 13:8-10 and 1 Corinthians 13. Indeed, the governmental way was so imperfect that for generations Christians did not believe they could in good conscience participate in it, as we will see in more detail in the next chapter.

Thus Paul's endorsement of governmental use of force in Romans 13 is not ringing. Taken in the context of the rest of Paul's writings and of the New Testament as a whole, Romans 13 only counsels Christians to submit to the authorities but does not allow them to participate in the state's unchristian actions. As such, it cannot be said that Romans 13 represents Paul's approval of the government's use of capital punishment.

The Government as the Beast

The persecution of the early church led to another perspective of the state, much less complimentary than Paul's view in Romans 13. This perspective is stated in Revelation 13. Here the government is symbolized as the beast, a creation of the devil. The beast has authority on the earth and demands to be worshiped in the place of God (Rev. 13:3-4). It uses its authority to control the lives of its citizens, mainly through economic policies (Rev. 13:16-17). Yet it also claims to have the authority of life and death over those it controls (Rev. 13:15).

This passage recognizes that the state can and will use capital punishment for its own purposes, not simply to maintain law and order. The New Testament churches, frequent victims of persecution, needed little reminder of this fact. As one by one the apostles were executed, it is hard to believe the early church did not question whether the death penalty was a useful tool for maintaining peace. Revelation's answer to this question is that the state has become a tool of Satan and works evil in a fallen world. The Roman empire demanded allegiance Christians could give only to God. Whenever the state does that, it uses the death penalty as its ultimate proselytizing tool.

Conclusion

Through his teaching and his actions, Jesus Christ showed his disapproval of capital punishment. Every execution that occurs in the New Testament is arbitrary and unjust. Christ himself stopped one execution and was the victim of another. These facts in and of themselves should lead Christians to view the death penalty unfavorably.

While early Christians recognized the need for the state to sometimes use force in restraining evil, their view was that the utility of force was limited and its use should be curtailed. The failure of the Christian community to endorse governmental violence made it highly suspect in the eyes of the Roman empire. This led to conflict with the government and to the martyrdom of many early Christians.

The New Testament shows that the earliest Christians viewed the death penalty primarily from the perspective of potential victims, not supporters or enforcers. As the next chapter will show, the subsequent history of the post-apostolic church reinforces the view that the earliest Christians opposed the death penalty and that this view came directly from their understanding that this was the position taken by Christ himself.

3
Opposition to the Death Penalty to 1700

The Early Church

Unfortunately, little scholarly work has been conducted on the history of opposition to the death penalty before 1700. However, it can be fairly said that the early Christian church was one of the first organized groups to speak against capital punishment.

Because Christians were not directly involved in the government and therefore did not have direct influence on governmental policy, direct statements about capital punishment are rare. However, we can deduce from statements made by the church and its leaders about war and violence in general that the church did oppose the death penalty.

This opposition was to some extent pragmatic. Early Christians were often the victims of persecution, and the death penalty was at times invoked against them because of their religious beliefs. However, opposition to capital punishment also stemmed from Christian doctrine derived from the life and death of Jesus. We have seen in the previous chapter that opposition to the death penalty in the New Testament can be logically derived from the doctrine of love and forgiveness preached by Christ.

However, can we be sure the early church came to this conclusion? Statements from early Christian apologists indicate that it did. These statements more often than not were about Christian participation in the military and more specifically in war, but at times the apologists also extended their condemnation of bloodshed to the condemnation of capital punishment. For example, Tertullian (160?-230?) wrote,

> Shall it be lawful to make an occupation of the sword when the Lord proclaims that he who lives by the sword shall perish by the sword? And shall the son of peace take part in the battle when it does not become him even to sue at law? And shall he apply the chain, and the prison, and the torture, and the punishment, who is not the avenger of even his own wrongs?[1]

Roland H. Bainton, in his classic study on *Christian Attitudes Toward War and Peace*, lists the following comments by early Christian theologians about bloodshed.

> In the West Tertullian declared that the Christian would rather be killed than to kill. For Minucius Felix, "It is not right for us to either see or hear a man being killed." Cyprian lamented that the world was wet with bloodshed and homicide esteemed a virtue if practiced publicly. Arnobius thought it better to pour out one's own blood than to stain one's hands and conscience with the blood of another. Lactantius declared that when God forbade killing he forbade not only brigandage but also that which is regarded as legal among men. . . . In the East Athenagoras said that the Christian cannot bear to see a man put to death even justly. Origen averred that "God did not deem it becoming to his own divine legislation to allow the killing of any man whatever." The Canons of Hippolytus enacted that a soldier of civil authority must be taught not to kill men and to refuse to do so if he is commanded.[2]

Statements from the early church are held in especially high regard by many Christians. These declarations are close to the source of Christianity in time and may represent the opinions of Christ himself as passed along to his earliest followers. Tertullian, for example, was only three or four generations removed from the apostles.

The Christian Roman Empire

While the earliest church was viewed as an outlaw organization by the Roman empire, gradually Christianity became first permissible, then accepted, and finally mandated by the empire. The church's acceptance of military participation is usually dated from the reign of the Emperor Constantine (288?-337), but Bainton points to evidence that the church was slowly adopting a more permissive attitude toward military service before that time.[3]

As the church became more involved with the functions of the state, it began to adopt many of the values of the state. The acceptance of capital punishment as a legitimate tool of government was one of those values. It was Augustine of Hippo (354-430) who provided the theological justification for this acceptance. Augustine maintained the early church's position that the state was a necessary evil. But according to Augustine, the church and the state should be partners in governance, with the state answerable to the church.[4] Since the church now had responsibility for governance, it at least in part had to sanction the actions of the state.

Regarding capital punishment, Augustine wrote,

> However, there are some exceptions made by divine authority to its own law, that men may not be put to death. . . . He to whom authority is delegated, and who is but a sword in the hand of him who uses it, is not himself responsible for the death he deals. . . . They who have waged war in obedience to the divine command, or in conformity with His laws have represented in their persons the public justice or the wisdom of the government, and in this capacity have put to death wicked men; such persons have by no means violated the commandment, "Thou shall not kill."[5]

Thus the church's alliance with the state led to the Christian acceptance of capital punishment. With the state as its champion, the church began to use the same methods to enforce its orthodoxy that had been used against the early Christians.[6]

The church's sanction for capital punishment was never without reservations, however. Until the time of the Reformation, the church continued to draw a distinct line between the functions of the church and the state. The church might sanction capital punishment, but it was to be the state that carried it out. By canon law church officials could not be involved in the actual execution. *"Ecclesia abhoret a sanguine"* (the church shrinks from bloodshed).

In addition, the church continued to place limits on how and when the death penalty could be used. Based on the Old Testament concept of cities of refuge, the church offered sanctuary for the accused within the walls of church buildings. Beginning in 615 the church also protected its own officials from capital charges through the concept of the benefit of clergy, a privilege which over the centuries came to be applied to anyone who could read.[7]

Medieval Opposition to Capital Punishment

While the death penalty received almost unanimous support during the Middle Ages, there were occasional pockets of opposition. One surprising opponent was William the Conqueror. He ordered that no person be put to death, no matter what the crime. William Rufus also refused to use the death penalty. The opposition of these kings, however, had more to do with their need for soldiers than any moral repugnance to killing.[8]

True opposition to the death penalty came from sectarians who often faced capital punishment for their religious views. One of the heresies charged against the Waldenses, for example, was their refusal to sanction any state punishment of criminals. "They teach that no judge may condemn anyone to any punishment, to which they adduce that it is written, 'Judge not, that ye be not judged.' " Writing a history of Anabaptism in the seventeenth century, Thieleman van Braght quoted this accusation but then claimed it was too broad and that the Waldenses only went so far as to condemn the use of the death penalty.[9]

The Reformation

While the Reformation did much to change the theology of many Christians, it did little to change the majority view of the alliance of the church and state, which supported the death penalty. Mainstream Reformers justified capital punishment within their theologies.

However, groups among the more radical Reformation factions, particularly those who felt the church should separate itself from the state, did come to the conclusion that capital punishment was wrong. As with the early Christians, such opposition was rooted in the gospel of grace and perhaps came partly because the death penalty was so frequently used on their members. It is estimated, for example, that 5,000 or more Anabaptists were put to death during the sixteenth century for their religious beliefs.

Written in 1527, the Schleitheim Confession of the Swiss Brethren Anabaptist group stated that the government might use the sword to punish and kill the wicked, but no true Christian could participate in this activity.

> Now many, who do not understand Christ's will for us, will ask: whether a Christian may or should use the sword against the wicked for the protection and defense of the good, or for the sake of love. The answer is unanimously revealed: Christ teaches and commands us to learn from Him, for He is meek and lowly of heart and thus we shall find rest for our souls. Now Christ says to the woman who was taken in adultery, not that she should be stoned according to the law of his Father (and yet He says, "what the Father commanded me, that I do") but with mercy and forgiveness and the warning to sin no more, says: "Go, sin no more." Exactly thus should we also proceed, according to the rule of the ban.[10]

A century later the government of the city of Berne in Switzerland justified its persecution of the Anabaptists in part for their failure to support the criminal justice system.

> Since the magistery . . . is given of God as an avenger, upon those that do evil, especially upon murderers, traitors, and the

like, the subjects are bound to make the same known to the authorities; but those who will not obligate themselves to do this, cannot be reckoned among the faithful and obedient subjects; now therefore as the Anabaptists are such as refuse to make known one of them to the authorities, they cannot be tolerated.[11]

Perhaps it was the use of the death penalty to enforce religious intolerance that led to a more general questioning of capital punishment. From this point in history, opposition to the death penalty was not only to grow but to be approached from a different direction. Although opposition to the death penalty continued to come chiefly from religious motives, new voices were beginning to question the usefulness of capital punishment for society. These voices did not necessarily oppose the death penalty in general but did question its use for certain nonlethal crimes. About 1520, the great Renaissance humanist Erasmus of Rotterdam wrote,

The civil magistrate, likewise, would act more judiciously, by employing upon public works criminals convicted of certain kinds of theft, or other offenses (which though in themselves heinous, are too light—especially in countries professing Christianity—to be punished with death) than by subjecting them to ignominious stigmas or mutilations. As of old, debtors in bonds served their creditors; others dug, chained, in the fields, or hewed timber; and a third class, accustomed to sedentary occupations, were confined to labor in workhouses. Punishments of this description are attended with a double advantage: for, while they correct, without crushing the offender, they promote the interests either of the public, or of the individual injured by his delinquency.[12]

Erasmus' friend, Sir Thomas More, later executed for his religious convictions, wrote about executing common thieves:

This way of punishing thieves, was neither just in itself, nor good for the public; for the severity was too great, so the remedy was not effectual: simple theft not being so great a crime, that it ought to cost a man his life; no punishment how severe soever, being able to restrain from robbing, who can find out no other way of livelihood.[13]

Although Erasmus and More were religious men, these statements of opposition to the death penalty were based primarily on social rather than religious considerations. This was the beginning of secular opposition to the death penalty, which then flowered in the eighteenth century. In that century, the opposition to capital punishment which was once largely religious and based on biblical principles became more practical.

This opposition (covered in more detail in the next chapter) emphasized more pragmatic, social reasons for abolishing the death penalty. Such arguments have an important influence on religious thinking about the death penalty as well. Therefore, while Christian opposition to capital punishment continued to be vitally important to the movement from the eighteenth century on, secular and religious opposition to the death penalty must be treated together.

4
Modern Opposition to the Death Penalty

"It was the best of times; it was the worst of times." This is how the great Victorian novelist Charles Dickens described the eighteenth century. Such a description was certainly true regarding capital punishment. In eighteenth-century England, the number of capital crimes rose first to 160 and then to 222 before reforms began. Most of these crimes were not crimes against persons, but crimes against property. These included thefts of goods from a house or shop, counterfeiting the stamps used on perfume or hair powder, robbing a rabbit warren, or cutting down a tree.[1]

Even more horrifying, capital punishment in England and other places was used on children as young as eight. On one occasion ten children under age ten were hanged together. As late as 1831, a boy of nine was hanged. Not until 1908 were executions of children under fourteen outlawed in England.[2]

Against this background, the first modern opposition to capital punishment arose. This opposition to the death penalty might also be termed "scientific," because the new death penalty opponents did not appeal so much to religious principles as they did to the social consequences of the death penalty. They contended that capital punishment was ineffective as a social tool. They set out to prove this, not through appeals to the Bible or to church doctrine, but to the newly developing psychological and social sciences.

Cesare Beccaria

One of the first influential modern opponents to capital punishment was Cesare Beccaria, an Italian criminologist. In 1764, at the age of twenty-six, he published *Essay on Crimes and Punishments*, a book which spoke against both capital punishment and the cruel treatment of criminals.

Beccaria felt that the death penalty was immoral, but more importantly, he believed it was ineffective. To prove his contention, Beccaria appealed both to history and psychology. He argued that psychologically, life imprisonment at hard labor would be a more effective deterrent to crime than capital punishment.

> It is not the intenseness of the pain that has the greatest effect on the mind, but its continuance; for our sensibility is more easily and more powerfully affected by weak but repeated impressions, than by a violent, but momentary impulse. . . . The death of a criminal is a terrible but momentary spectacle, and therefore a less efficacious method of deterring others, than the continued example of a man deprived of his liberty, condemned, as a beast of burden, to repair, by his labor, the injury he has done to society. *If I commit such a crime,* says the spectator to himself, *I shall be reduced to that miserable condition for the rest of my life.*[3]

Beccaria went on to say,

> Perpetual slavery, then, has in it all that is necessary to deter the most hardened and determined, as much as the punishment of death. I say it has more. There are many who look upon death with intrepidity and firmness; some through fanaticism, and others through vanity, which attends us even to the grave; others from a desperate resolution, either to get rid of their misery, or cease to live; but fanaticism and vanity forsake the criminal in slavery, in chains and fetters, in an iron cage; and despair seems rather the beginning than the end of their misery.

Beccaria also argued that capital punishment had a brutalizing effect on society.

The punishment of death is pernicious to society, from the example of barbarity that it affords. If the passions, or the necessity of war, have taught men to shed the blood of their fellow creatures, the laws, which are intended to moderate the ferocity of mankind, should not increase it by examples of barbarity, the more horrible, as this punishment is usually attended with formal pageantry. Is it not absurd, that the laws, which detest and punish homicide, should, in order to prevent murder, publicly commit murder themselves?

Beccaria also pointed out the common feelings of revulsion held toward executioners. If people really thought that this kind of killing was morally correct, he questioned, why would they regard executioners with aversion rather than respect?

Beccaria related the use of the death penalty to despotic tendencies in government. At the same time he claimed that the death penalty might actually encourage violence rather than prevent it.

What must men think, when they see wise magistrates and grave ministers of justice, with indifference and tranquillity, dragging a criminal to death, and whilst a wretch trembles with agony, expecting the fatal stroke, the judge, who has condemned him, with the coldest insensibility, and perhaps with no small gratification from the exertion of his authority, quits his tribunal to enjoy the comforts and pleasures of life. They will say,

Ah! those cruel formalities of justice are a cloak of tyranny, they are a secret language, a solemn veil, intended to conceal the sword by which we are sacrificed to the insatiable idol of despotism. Murder, which they represent to us as an horrible crime, we see practiced by them without repugnance, or remorse. Let us follow their example. A violent death appeared terrible in their descriptions, but we see that it is the affair of a moment. It will be less terrible to him, who is not expecting it, [since he] escapes almost all the pain.

The work of Cesare Beccaria introduced a number of themes that were to be repeated by many modern opponents of the death penalty. The first and perhaps most important was that the death penalty did not deter crime.

The second was that the death penalty might actually induce crime rather than deter it, largely because of its brutalizing effects on society.

The last argument was that the death penalty was closely aligned with those who would create a more tyrannical society.

It is important to remember that Beccaria was writing shortly before the beginning of the American and the French revolutions. At that time the concept of liberty was an increasingly important element of political theory in Europe.

Cruel and Unusual Punishment

These "winds of liberty" were to have important effects on the political writers who created the Constitution of the United States and particularly its first ten amendments, the Bill of Rights. In addition to providing for due process in criminal cases, in the Eighth Amendment the Constitution prohibited "cruel and unusual punishments." The founding fathers did not feel that they were prohibiting capital punishment with this clause. Instead, they were trying to stop torture and inhumane methods of execution, such as burning at the stake.

This was a step in the direction of death penalty abolition, however, and the constitutional phrase has been used by later interpreters of the Constitution as an argument against the death penalty. For if death is not a cruel and unusual punishment, they were to argue, what is?

Fyodor Dostoyevsky, the great Russian novelist and one of a number of important writers who opposed the death penalty, wrote powerfully about the cruelty of capital punishment. Dostoyevsky, who had been a prisoner in Siberia, had actually faced death by firing squad. Only at the last moment was he untied from the stake and his sentence commuted. Based on his experience, he wrote a description of the condemned person's last moments in his novel *The Idiot*, published in 1869.

> Yet the chief and the worst pain is perhaps not inflicted by wounds, but by your certain knowledge that in an hour, in ten minutes, in half a minute, now, this moment, your soul will fly out

of your body, and that you will be a human being no longer, and that that's certain—the main thing is that it is *certain*. Just when you lay your head under the knife and you hear the swish of the knife as it slides down over your head—it is just that fraction of a second that is the most awful of all. . . . To kill for murder is an immeasurably greater evil than the crime itself. Murder by legal process is immeasurably more dreadful than murder by a brigand. A man who is murdered by brigands is killed at night in a forest or somewhere else, and up to the last moment he still hopes that he will be saved. . . . But here all this last hope, which makes it ten times easier to die, is taken away *for certain*; here you have been sentenced to death, and the whole terrible agony lies in the fact that you will most certainly not escape, and there is no agony greater than that. Take a soldier and put him in front of a cannon in battle and fire at him and he will still hope, but read the same soldier his death sentence *for certain*, and he will go mad and burst out crying. Who says that human nature is capable of bearing this without madness? Why this cruel, hideous, and unnecessary mockery? . . . It was of agony like this and of such horror that Christ spoke. No, you can't treat a man like that![4]

Executing the Innocent

Another powerful argument against capital punishment made by the modern opponents was that innocent people could be executed. The Marquis de Lafayette, the French nobleman who fought with the American Army in the Revolutionary War, is reported to have said, "I shall ask for abolition of the punishment of death until I have the infallibility of human judgment demonstrated to me." And François Robespierre, who later became a victim of the guillotine himself in the French Revolution, declared,

> Listen to the voice of justice and of reason. It tells us that human judgments are never so certain as to permit society to kill a human being judged by other human beings. . . . Why deprive ourselves of any chance to redeem such errors? Why condemn yourselves to helplessness when faced with persecuted innocence?[5]

The power of this contention can be seen in a speech made by the philosopher John Stuart Mill to the British Parliament in 1868. Mill was arguing for retaining the death penalty for murder.

> There is one argument against capital punishment, even in extreme cases, which I cannot deny to have weight. . . . It is this—that if by an error of justice an innocent person is put to death, the mistake can never be corrected; all compensation, all reparation for the wrong is impossible. This would be indeed a serious objection if these miserable mistakes—among the most tragical occurrences in the whole round of human affairs—could not be made extremely rare. The argument is invincible where the mode of criminal procedure is dangerous to the innocent, or where the Courts of Justice are not trusted.[6]

The Brutalizing Effect

Mill went on to argue that the criminal justice system in England was good enough to keep unjust executions from occurring. However, the contention that the criminal justice system in England was somehow more perfect than those of other countries was belied by the way public executions were carried out. These executions and the behavior they instilled in the crowds who attended them became a powerful point of attack for death penalty opponents until public executions were eliminated in 1868. William Makepeace Thackeray, the great Victorian novelist, wrote these impressions of a public hanging.

> In one of the houses near us, a gallery has been formed on the roof. Seats were let here and a number of persons of various degrees were occupying them. Several tipsy, dissolute-looking young men . . . were in this gallery. One was lolling over the sunshiny tiles, with a fierce sodden face, out of which came a pipe, and which was shaded by long matted hair, and a hat cocked very much on one side. This gentleman was one of a party which had evidently not gone to bed on Sunday night, but had passed it in some of the delectable night-houses in the neighborhood of Covent Garden. The debauch was not over yet, and the women of the party were giggling, drinking, and romping, as is the wont of

these delectable creatures; sprawling here and there, and falling on one or the other of the males. . . . I must confess that the sight has left on my mind an extraordinary feeling of terror and shame. It seems to me that I have been abetting an act of frightful wickedness and violence performed by a set of men against one of their fellows; and I pray God that it may soon be out of the power of any man in England to witness such a hideous and degrading sight. Forty thousand persons (say the Sheriffs), of all ranks and degree—mechanics, gentlemen, pickpockets, members of both Houses of Parliament, streetwalkers, newspaper writers, gather together before Newgate at a very early hour; the most part of them give up their natural quiet night's rest in order to partake of this hideous debauchery, which is more exciting than sleep, or than wine, or the last new ballet, or any other amusement they can have. Pickpocket and Peer, each is tickled by the sight alike, and has that hidden lust after blood which influences our race. . . . I fully confess that I came away from Snow Hill that morning with a disgust for murder—but it was for the murder I saw done.[7]

Charles Dickens, who was so familiar with the degrading poverty of Victorian England, went even further in his comments.

The effect of public executions on those who witness them, requires no better illustration, and can have none, than the scene which any execution in itself presents, and the general Police-office knowledge of the offenses arising out of them. I have stated my belief that the study of such scenes leads to a disregard for human life, and to murder. Referring since that expression of opinion to the very last trial for murder in London, I have made inquiry, and am assured that the youth now under sentence of death in Newgate for the murder of his master in Drury Lane, was a vigilant spectator of the three last executions in this city.[8]

The Beginnings of Abolition

These arguments against capital punishment had important effects over the two hundred years following the publication of Beccaria's *Essay on Crimes and Punishments*. In 1823 Great Britain passed legislation that removed about 100 crimes from the list of those punishable by death, and by 1860 over 190 offenses had been reduced to the status of noncapital crimes.

In France the number of capital offenses was reduced from 115 to thirty between 1789 and 1871. Some countries, such as Belgium and Finland, while not formally abolishing capital punishment during this period, no longer carried out executions. And the death penalty was abolished in a number of countries: Portugal (1867), Holland (1870), Romania (1870), Italy (1888), Norway (1905), Austria (1919), and Sweden (1921).[9]

Changes in the political climate caused some countries to reinstate the death penalty. Thus under Mussolini, Italy reestablished capital punishment in 1928; Italy abolished it again after World War II ended.

Since the end of that war, many nations have abolished the death penalty, either for all crimes or at least for all crimes during peacetime. In 1996 only the United States and Japan, of all the developed nations, still maintain and use the punishment of death.

American Opposition to Capital Punishment

The stubborn retention of capital punishment in the United States is grimly ironic. Born of the same Enlightenment ideas that brought forth the modern opposition to capital punishment, the United States, during its first hundred years, was on the cutting edge of death penalty abolition. Part of this attitude came from the influence of the Quakers in Pennsylvania, who for religious reasons opposed the death penalty. The Royal Charter for this colony listed only premeditated murder as a capital crime. For thirty years Pennsylvania remained an "abolitionist" colony. However, later demands from Great Britain forced Pennsylvania to use the harsh British criminal code in the eighteenth century.

The father of the modern anti-capital punishment movement in the United States was Benjamin Rush, a medical doctor and a signer of the Declaration of Independence. Rush was influenced by Beccaria's *Essay on Crimes and Punishments*. He advocated the use of humane penitentiaries in place of the death penalty. In such penitentiaries, Rush claimed, criminals would be rehabilitated, while society would be protected.

Because of the influence of such men as Rush, Benjamin Franklin, and state attorney general William Bradford, Pennsylvania eliminated capital punishment for all crimes except first-degree murder in 1794.[10] Edward Livingston, an attorney, became one of the primary leaders of the movement for death penalty abolition in the early nineteenth century. Anti-capital punishment organizations, referred to as "anti-gallows societies," were formed primarily in the east.

As a result of these influences, in 1846 Michigan became the first state to abolish the death penalty. Other states that joined Michigan in abolishing the death penalty in the nineteenth century were Rhode Island, Wisconsin, Iowa (briefly), Maine, and Colorado (briefly).

Full abolition was not the only reform that death penalty advocates worked for during these years. Many states limited the number of crimes punishable by death. By the time of the Civil War, most northern states retained only murder and treason as capital crimes, with a few others that varied from state to state. In the South the code was harsher, but even there the number of capital crimes was reduced.[11]

In some states, the major reform was to move capital punishment from a mandatory sentence to a discretionary sentence. Tennessee (1838), Alabama (1841), and Louisiana (1846) were among the first states to move in this direction. Twenty more joined them by the end of the nineteenth century.

Another somewhat contradictory aim was to make executions more humane. Other less-painful methods of execution were advocated: the electric chair, the gas chamber, and more recently lethal injection.

The movement for abolition of the death penalty in the United States has ebbed and flowed. Generally, during times of social stress, such as wars and economic depressions, movement has been away from abolition. During times of peace and prosperity, the abolitionist movement has fared better. In the first two decades of the twentieth century, for example, nine states—Kansas, Minnesota, Washington, Oregon, North Dakota, South Dakota, Tennessee, Arizona, and Missouri abolished capital punishment, at least for a time. Significantly, four of these states returned to the death penalty either during or immediately after the United States' brief involvement in the First World War. The 1960s were another period when states began to move away from capital punishment. During the times of World War I, the Great Depression, and World War II, on the other hand, little progress was made toward eliminating capital punishment.[12]

With the civil rights movement of the 1950s and 1960s, the death penalty issue became increasingly discussed in terms of race. It had become apparent that the imposition of the death penalty was frequently determined by the offender's race. In 1972 the United States Supreme Court issued a landmark decision in the case of Furman versus Georgia. The court held that the existing death penalty laws did not provide sufficient guidance to judges and juries to decide when to impose the death penalty. The decision voided all the death penalty statutes then on the books, essentially ending capital punishment in the United States.

Then in 1976 in the case of Gregg versus Georgia, the court held that new statutes which *did* provide adequate standards and procedures for fairly imposing the death sentence were constitutional. Thirty-eight states have rewritten their death penalty statutes to meet the Supreme Court standards.

Since that time, the Supreme Court has made numerous rulings on death penalty cases. The general trend in these rulings has been to uphold death penalty conviction and to lessen avenues of appeal. As this book is being written, there are over 3,000 men and women on America's death rows.

Conclusion

While the current time might be a discouraging one for death penalty opponents, the historical perspective is more encouraging. In general, it is clear that the historical trend in the West is away from the death penalty. With the exception of the

United States and Japan, all developed nations have eliminated capital punishment during peacetime. In America fewer crimes are punishable by death, the death penalty is no longer imposed on young children, and there are no longer mandatory death sentences. Public support for the death penalty continues to be high, but the long-term worldwide trend has been toward abolition.

The quality of the people who have spoken against the death penalty over the years is also impressive. Beginning with the partial abolitionists, including Erasmus, Thomas More, Voltaire, Benjamin Franklin, Samuel Johnson, and Oliver Goldsmith; and then the full abolitionists, including Charles Dickens, Victor Hugo, William Makepeace Thackeray, Fyodor Dostoyevsky, Horace Greeley, William Randolph Hearst, Clarence Darrow, Aldous Huxley, Albert Camus, and Mohandas Gandhi—we find some of the most important social thinkers and literary figures of the modern era. Historically, capital punishment abolitionists stand in good company.

Abolition of the death penalty, more than any other reform, appears to occur in stages. Abolitionists have been able to use the most obvious injustices and cruelties to gain a foothold in the public's conscience. These small victories have led to greater sensitivity to other death penalty issues.

Polls show the death penalty to have broad support from the American public, but this support is not deep. When offered a "true" life sentence without possibility of parole as an alternative to capital punishment, support for the death penalty plummets. Similarly, there appears to be little support for executing offenders who are proved to be mentally retarded, and there are strong doubts about executing juveniles.

In general, it appears that many people support capital punishment without thinking much about it. When learning more about how capital punishment is applied and other issues surrounding capital punishment, many people rethink their position. In following chapters, information about all these issues will be given.

5
Deterrence?
Social and Psychological
Factors Say No

One of the most frequent arguments made in favor of capital punishment is that the imposition of the death penalty on some criminals deters other criminals from committing capital offenses. In using this argument, death penalty proponents make certain assumptions, such as the following:

1. That all people reason in the same way.
2. That the decision to commit a murder is a reasonable decision in which the potential murderer carefully weighs the potential consequences of the act.
3. That potential murderers are aware that capital punishment exists, and that the risk of being executed if they commit a murder is high.
4. That potential murderers fear being executed.

It is doubtful, however, that these assumptions are true in many murders, if any.

Criminal Thinking

By definition, a criminal is someone who does not fit into the acceptable range of normal behavior. Criminals behave differently than normal people. Since behavior is based to some extent on how we think, it is safe to say that people likely to commit capital crimes also think differently from normal people. Indeed, one of the current movements in the treatment of prison inmates is to provide them with training about "thinking errors."

The *Volunteer Orientation Packet* published by the Idaho Department of Corrections describes this thinking.

> Offenders often think they are entitled to a kind of absolute freedom in the way they conduct their lives. They may picture themselves as living in isolation from the world, in a kind of world of their own. In their subjective world, they are in absolute control and have the absolute right to do as they please. From this point of view, any restriction of their freedom is resented as an unjust intrusion.
>
> When the real world fails to comply with their expectations and demands, they take a stance of righteous defiance. Relationships with other people are dominated by the struggle for power. . . . Righteous anger, retribution, and license to do as they please, *without regard to rules or consequences* [my emphasis], become dominant themes of living.[1]

In addition to this basic cognitive stance of many criminals, other psychological factors that prevent punishment of any kind—and capital punishment in particular—from deterring crime are these: belief that violence is normal, drug and alcohol abuse, suicidal tendencies, mental illness, mental retardation, and other undiagnosed disabling conditions.

The Normalcy of Violence

In my personal work with prison inmates, I have found that among inmates violence is considered a normal part of life rather than an occasional aberration. Many have reported that as children they were abused—physically, sexually, or both. There is also empirical evidence for this contention. A 1988 study of fourteen juvenile death row inmates, for example, found that twelve had been physically abused as children. Five had been sodomized by relatives.[2]

The story of Robert Alton Harris, the first man to be executed in California after the Furman decision, is not unusual in this regard. Harris' mother was an alcoholic. He was born three months premature after his father repeatedly kicked his mother. As a child he was frequently beaten by his father and at times choked until he went into convulsions. His father also threatened to shoot him. As the result of this family history, Harris suffered from fetal alcohol syndrome and an organic brain disorder, in the opinion of experts.[3]

Many death row inmates entered the criminal justice system early in life. Violence is normative in institutions for youthful offenders and prisons. In such settings failure to react violently to conflict situations is seen as weakness. Many offenders have also come from neighborhoods that are exceptionally violent—where homicide may be the leading cause of death.[4] With this background, many have only limited experience with nonviolent methods for working through conflict.

Some murderers are members of criminal gangs. The strong social sanction for violence found in gangs may override any other inhibition against it. Murder may then become a way of gaining status in the gang. For young men or women who find their whole social meaning in their gang membership, this need for acceptance will often counteract any fear about potentially negative consequences of their behavior.

If violence is understood to be an everyday occurrence, and if it is even seen as a way of achieving social status in some groups, then the death penalty can do little to deter murder. Instead, the chance of being executed will be seen as one more relatively minor risk in a very risky life. This is especially true if a person's means of livelihood comes from a criminal activity, such as selling drugs. Indeed, if one is involved in this kind of crime, the chances of being executed (if the criminal thinks of this possibility at all), will be considered much less probable than being killed in some other fashion.[5]

Drug and Alcohol Abuse as a Factor in Murder

The deterrence theorists assume that murderers make rational decisions about homicidal activities. This implies that murderers must be in control of their mental faculties when the murder occurs. If murderers are not in control of their emotions and reasoning ability, then the deterrence theory cannot be true.

Drug or alcohol abuse, of course, weakens a person's ability to make good choices based on reason. Drugs or alcohol distorts a person's perception of reality. The inhibitions of such a person may be lowered; they may have a false sense of their own abilities. Drugs and alcohol can intensify feelings of anger. This can lead to violence.

Therefore it is significant that most people who are arrested for murder were using drugs or alcohol or both at the time of their crime. In a 1989 study drug tests were made on 263 men and 37 women arrested for homicide. Tests were made for the following drugs: cocaine, opiates, marijuana, PCP's, Valium, Quaaludes, Darvon, barbiturates, and amphetamines. It was found that 57 percent of the males and 46 percent of the females tested positive for drug use.[6] Another 1989 study found that fully 68.7 percent of 3,912 people convicted for homicide had been under the influence of drugs (5.5%), alcohol (49.5%), or both (13.7%) at the time of their offense.[7]

Given that drug or alcohol use may be a factor in nearly 70 percent of all murders, it is doubtful that these murderers will be affected much by the existence or the nonexistence of the death penalty. People under the influence of these substances are not likely to stop and think about their actions. Even if they do, they may not be able to resist their violent impulses.

Suicidal Tendencies

One Idaho murderer told investigators shortly after his arrest that he wanted to die. "It's time for the evil in my body to be put to rest," he said.[8]

This statement seems to fit a pattern fairly common in death penalty cases. Suicidal tendencies on the part of criminals lead them to commit a murder in hopes of receiving the death penalty. In these cases the state actually becomes the instrument of suicide. Murder of the victim is merely the method by which the criminal gets the state to act.

One well-known case of this kind was that of Pamela Watkins, a California woman. After several failed suicide attempts, she killed two children in her care in hopes of receiving a death sentence.[9] Gary Gilmore also fit the murder-suicide pattern. He was executed by firing squad in Utah in 1977 after refusing to appeal his sentence (thus becoming the first person to be executed after the Furman decision). In fact, 26 (13%) of the 199 men and women executed between 1977 and April 20, 1993, gave up their appeals and were executed voluntarily.[10]

How common are death row suicidal tendencies? Suicide prevention is a major issue for death row administrators. Measures are taken to assure that death row inmates do not have access to objects that could be used for committing suicide. Despite these extraordinary precautions and around-the-clock supervision, there were 36 successful suicides between January 1, 1972, and April 20, 1993.[11] This gives death row inmates an annual suicide rate of roughly 63 per 100,000 population.[12] The suicide rate for white men in 1989 was 21.4 per 100,000, and the suicide rate for African-American men was 12.2 per 100,000.[13]

In other words, the suicide rate of death row inmates, conservatively figured, was three times greater than the rate for white males in the general population and five times greater than the rate for African-American males. The high stress of life on death row may account for some suicide attempts, and the preference to die at one's own hand rather than be executed may play a role. Yet whatever the reasons, death row inmates tend to be much more suicidal than people in the general population.

For someone who is suicidal, the death penalty will not act as a deterrent, since the person is seeking death. Indeed the death penalty may actually induce an unstable person to commit a murder in hopes of receiving a death sentence.

Mental Illness

Mental illness is "the state of having severely disordered behavior, thoughts or feelings, usually taken to exclude cases where the disorder arises from low intelligence or as a result of strokes or other direct brain injury."[14] Mental illness is a disability that causes a person to perceive and react to the world in a way not validated by objective data. Such illness creates serious difficulties in relating to other people.

By definition, a mentally ill person will not react to an event in the same way as people who are "normal." People who are mentally ill, for example, may experience paranoid feelings about others. They may think others are threatening them or their family. They may react to these feelings with violence against the person or persons they perceive to be threatening. They may also hear voices, as in the Son of Sam case, that order them to kill.

Brain Injury

Direct brain injuries, although not considered a mental illness, can result in symptoms that are similar. Therefore, it is significant that one study of fourteen juvenile death row inmates conducted in 1988 found that all had received head injuries as children.[15]

While the percentage of people who are mentally ill or brain injured and who also commit crimes is quite low, those criminals who are mentally ill or brain injured are not likely to interpret an execution in the same way as a normal person. Executions may exacerbate feelings of paranoia or be interpreted as a message that justifies one's own violence or intended violence. Thus the death penalty is not likely to deter a potential murderer suffering from mental illness or brain injury.

Mental Retardation

About 10 percent of the men and women on death row are mentally retarded. Mental retardation is a condition that affects a person's ability to reason, understand, and communicate.

Mentally retarded people are not likely to have an understanding of what capital punishment means or how it might affect them if they commit a crime. Moreover, they are prone to behave more impulsively, to act without thinking through what their behavior may mean. (A fuller discussion of the effects of mental retardation appears in chapter ten.)

James Ellis, president of the American Association on Mental Retardation, testified before the U.S. Congress in support of a bill that would prohibit the execution of mentally retarded defendants in federal cases. He stated that it was "implausible" that a mentally retarded person would be more likely to commit a crime because he could not be executed.[16]

Other Disabling Conditions

In recent years, psychologists have come to understand the importance that a number of conditions, undiagnosed in the past, may play in the behavior patterns of individuals. Perhaps the most important of these is attention deficit disorder (ADD). ADD hinders an individual's ability to concentrate. It may also be associated with hyperactivity (ADHD) and be related to impulsivity, venturesomeness, and risk-taking—all associated with criminal behavior in psychological studies.[17] Thus ADHD can have a major impact on an individual's ability to relate well in social situations. Undiagnosed ADHD may lead to failure in school, family difficulties, and general problems in relating to authority. All of these conditions, of course, may also contribute to criminal behaviors.

Again, a potential murderer with ADHD is not likely to be affected by the existence of the death penalty. Impulsivity would lead such persons to act without thinking. Their risk-taking behaviors may even lead them to see the possibility of being executed as a challenge rather than a deterrent to committing a capital crime.

Conclusion

The deterrence argument for capital punishment begins with the idea that potential murderers have the ability to think through their behavior before it is carried out and rationally to relate their behavior to its possible consequences. This theory assumes first that criminals know capital punishment exists, that they consider what the existence of capital punishment may mean for them, and that they are indeed afraid of being executed.

In this chapter a number of factors have been shown to make these assumptions unlikely in most murder cases. Criminal thinking errors, abusive backgrounds, environments and subcultures that normalize or exult violence, impulsivity, risk-taking and venturesomeness, and substance abuse—some or all of these appear to be factors in the behavior of almost all murderers. Often a combination of these factors is present. The presence of such factors makes it unlikely that many murders would be prevented because the potential murderer is afraid of being executed.

Most murders, even premeditated murders, are acts of passion. In order to kill, people must have an overriding anger. Even then, in over half the cases, they must be drugged or drunk to carry out the act. The reasons for a murder may be traceable to the relationship between the murderer and the victim or may be related to experiences the murderer brings to the situation. The murder of a complete stranger is caused by the murderer's inability to deal appropriately with his own psychological past, or with the changes in his brain chemistry. In these cases, the victim simply is a stand-in for the person or persons causing the murderer's anger.

With this in mind, we see that capital punishment cannot serve as a deterrent. If people are so angry that they desire to kill, it seems doubtful that they will be able to carefully perform the social or moral calculus required for the death penalty to deter them from murder.

6
Deterrence?
Statistics Say No

Early in the era of scientific opposition to capital punishment, death penalty abolitionists began to search for empirical evidence to bolster their case. Statistical studies of homicide rates became increasingly important as the debate on capital punishment continued. The studies became increasingly sophisticated.[1]

Two basic types of statistical studies have been made. The first, called a cross-sectional analysis, compares the homicide rate in jurisdictions that use capital punishment with those which do not. The assumption of this kind of study is that if capital punishment deters crime, then (all other things being equal) the murder rate in jurisdictions with capital punishment should be lower than in jurisdictions without the death penalty.

The second kind of study, called a time-series analysis, examines the murder rate before and after a significant change in death penalty policy or after significant death penalty events, such as a well-publicized sentencing or execution. The assumption of this kind of study is that if the death penalty deters murder, then (all other things being equal) the homicide rate should decrease after death penalty laws are strengthened, after well-publicized death sentences are handed down, or after executions are carried out.

Probably the first application of statistical data was the unsophisticated use of raw statistics. Statistics of one state or nation that used capital punishment were compared to another that did not use the death penalty. Such comparisons are still made. For example, death penalty opponents are fond of pointing out that the states that most often use the death penalty are also states that have higher than average murder rates. Most of the abolitionist states have lower than average homicide rates. Similarly, death penalty opponents often point to the high murder rate in the United States compared to other developed countries, none of which retain the death penalty. They take this as evidence that capital punishment does not deter crime. Such comparisons lack statistical validity but probably created interest in the more sophisticated use of statistical studies.

Cross-sectional Studies

The first important study was conducted by Robert Rantoul Jr. in 1846. In studies that combined elements of cross-sectional analysis and time-series analysis, Rantoul examined murder rates in England, France, Prussia, Belgium, and Saxony over a number of years. He compared the rates with the number of executions. Based on his analysis of the data, he found that the death penalty appeared to incite rather than deter murders. This theory has come to be known as the brutalization theory.

As statistical data improved, more studies were conducted. In 1919 Raymond Bye compared the murder rates for the years 1906-1915 for states that had abolished capital punishment with neighboring states that had retained it. By using neighboring states rather than all other states, Bye's study made an attempt to control for other factors that might affect murder rates. Bye found that all but one of the seven abolitionist states he studied had a lower homicide rate than neighboring states that had retained capital punishment.

Similar studies conducted by G. B. Old in 1932 and 1952, K. F. Schuessler in 1952, and Thorsten Sellin in 1959, all showed similar results. In 1969, W. C. Reckless, in a somewhat more sophisticated study, paired abolitionist and retentionist states based on similarities in other statistical characteristics. Of the nine pairs of states studied, five of the abolitionist states had a lower murder rate than its pair, three of the retentionist states had a lower rate, and one pair of states had equal murder rates.

Time-Series Studies

In 1935 Robert Dann conducted a time-series study to discover the short-term effects of execution. Dann examined the homicide rate in Philadelphia sixty days before and sixty days after well-publicized executions were carried out in 1927, 1929, 1930, 1931, and 1932. He found that the number of murders *increased* after the executions. Dann's work did not take into account the effect of season on the murder rate. However, later researchers, who controlled for seasonal differences, found the number of murders following the executions to be higher than expected.[2]

Dann's study inspired a number of similar studies. William Graves checked Los Angeles, San Francisco, and Alameda County murder rates following executions in 1946-1955. Leonard Savitz studied Philadelphia murder rates after well-publicized death sentences imposed in 1944, 1946 (two), and 1947. David King analyzed murder rates in South Carolina following 20 well publicized executions in 1951-1962. William J. Bowers and Glenn Pierce scrutinized monthly homicide statistics for New York in 1906-1963. William Bailey explored homicide data from Chicago for 1915-1921. All of these studies showed higher than expected increases in homicide rates immediately following well-publicized executions or death sentences.

Murders of Law Enforcement Officers

Statistical studies became increasingly more sophisticated in examining the effects of executions. One area that received a number of studies was the effect of capital punishment on the murder of police officers. Such murders are more likely to be treated as capital cases. Separate studies by Thorsten Sellin and by D. Campion in 1955 showed that the rate on police officers being murdered was generally lower in abolitionist states than in retentionist states. Sellin also performed a study of the murder of prison guards and prison inmates in 1967, which though yielding insufficient data to make reliable comparisons, showed no qualitative indications of deterrent effects.

William C. Bailey and Ruth D. Peterson conducted a sophisticated study, published in 1994, correlating the results of highly publicized executions and the number of murders of police officers. Again, there was no statistical evidence of a deterrent effect.

The Ehrlich Controversy and Other Pro-Deterrence Studies

Until the 1970s, no statistical study supported the theory that executions deter murder. This changed when Isaac Ehrlich published a study in 1975 that made a case for deterrence. Ehrlich used a sophisticated model that looked at the following variables: arrest rate in murder cases, conviction rate of murder arrests, the rate of labor force participation, the unemployment rate, the fraction of the population in the age-group from fourteen to twenty-four, and per capita income in addition to the murder rate and the number of executions.

Based on his analysis, Ehrlich concluded that "an additional execution per year . . . may have resulted in . . . seven or eight fewer murders." Ehrlich's work became especially important when his results were cited by the U.S. Solicitor General in a brief supporting capital punishment presented to the Supreme Court in the case of Fowler versus North Carolina.

While Ehrlich's work seemed to show statistically that capital punishment did indeed deter further murders, his study came under attack almost as soon as released. Statisticians Peter Passell and John Taylor found that the study held up only under certain restricted mathematical conditions. They also found that Ehrlich's findings were only true when one included the period 1962-1969, a time when few executions were carried out but also an era of severe social upheaval. They discovered that if the study was conducted only on the period 1933-1961, no deterrent effect was found. The work of Passell and Taylor was confirmed later by other researchers. A study similar to Ehrlich's, conducted on Canadian data from 1926 to 1960 by Kenneth Avio, found no evidence for the deterrence hypothesis.

Other scholars cited additional weaknesses in Ehrlich's study. They included his failure to distinguish statistics from states where the death penalty had been abolished and from those states where it had been retained, the dubious quality of Ehrlich's raw data, and numerous technical difficulties with Ehrlich's model. One critic of Ehrlich's study was Lawrence Klein, president of the American Economic Association. He concluded that his study team found "too many plausible explanations for his finding a deterrent effect other than the theory that capital punishment deters murder. . . . Ehrlich's results cannot be used at this time to pass judgment on the use of the death penalty."[3]

However, Stephen K. Layson, in a 1985 study which extended Ehrlich's study dates through 1977, claimed that his work not only confirmed Ehrlich's findings but made it appear deterrence was more pronounced than Ehrlich had estimated. Like Ehrlich's study, however, Layson's was also criticized on technical grounds.

In 1980 David Phillips published a study of homicide rates in London following the executions of well-known murderers during 1864-1921. Phillips claimed there was a statistically significant drop in murders the week immediately following a well-publicized execution. However, a "rebound" effect led to *more* murders in the weeks following. This made the total effect the same as if no execution had occurred. In reexamining Phillips' data and extending the expected effect period, however, William J. Bowers found that the immediate deterrent effect Phillips had found was illusory. The executions appeared to contribute to more murders rather than to deter them.

Finally, in 1987 S. Stack studied the 1950-1980 correspondence between print media attention to executions and the United States homicide rate. He also found evidence of deterrence in a fresh analysis of the study conducted by David King in South Carolina. However, as with the other studies which had shown a deterrent effect, another analysis of the Stack study, made by William Bailey and Ruth Peterson, found a number of problems. They included an unorthodox measure of the murder rate, the failure to include a number of significant

factors, and coding errors. When these problems were corrected, there was no evidence of deterrence.[4]

Conclusion

Neither statistical studies nor social and psychological factors lend support to the deterrence theory of capital punishment. Yet they lend some support to the theory that executions
may actually lead to a higher murder rate through the brutalization of society.

With few exceptions, social scientists appear to accept that
capital punishment has no deterrent effect on murder rates.
Those who support the death penalty as a way of reducing
crime have no uncontested scientific evidence for this claim.
Even police who have much more practical experience with
criminal behavior rate the death penalty low on a list of crime
preventive measures.[5]

All of this shows that the use of capital punishment does
not deter crime.

7

The Death Penalty and Repeat Offenders

Perhaps the strongest intellectual argument for capital punishment is that the death penalty prevents murderers from committing repeat offenses. The death penalty, it is argued, can save the innocent by making sure that the guilty cannot commit future crimes. This is a powerful contention, because it appeals to our need for safety and to our sense of revulsion at some crimes.

For example, the rape, torture, and murder of a child is not only repugnant to society but threatens all who are parents, since it brings into question the safety of their own children. Therefore it is easy to say that a person who commits such an act should be executed, not just because of the horrible thing he has done, but to make certain he never has opportunity to do it again.

It is also a powerful argument when the example used is of a murderer already under life sentence who has killed someone else, particularly a prison official, while serving his term. If the prison system cannot control this person, it is argued, then killing him may be the only way to protect society.

The assumption made by this argument for capital punishment is that there are no real alternatives. In reality, there are viable alternatives. These alternatives not only can protect society but also may provide better closure and restitution for victim families.

Offering Alternatives

Frequently death penalty opponents are considered "soft on crime" because they do not wish to kill criminals. It is not unusual to be asked, "How would you like to live next door to this murderer?" or "Why do you want these people out where they can kill again?" Such questions are unfair, since they make the assumption that society cannot be protected without capital punishment. This assumption is not true.

For example, one alternative to the death sentence is the life sentence without the possibility of parole. A 1993 poll conducted by the Democratic polling firm of Greenberg-Lake in conjunction with the Republican oriented Torrance Group showed that while 77 percent of the public supports the death penalty, support drops rapidly if alternatives are offered. Only 41 percent would continue to support the death penalty, for example, if an alternative of life without parole plus some restitution were available.[1] This confirms a number of other surveys taken over the years. See the chart on the next page.

This is not the place to discuss whether life without parole is the best way to treat criminals who would otherwise face the death penalty. Certainly there are less severe alternatives, such as life without possibility of parole for twenty-five or more years. The point is that there are alternatives to the death penalty. When those alternatives are offered, many people rethink their position on capital sentencing.

However, will society be truly safe from these inmates? It is standard prison knowledge that "lifers" tend to be among the most manageable of prisoners. A study in Alabama found that inmates serving a life-without-parole sentence committed only half the disciplinary offenses per capita of other prisoners. Wardens often look on lifers as model prisoners. Leo Lalonde of the Michigan Department of Corrections has stated, "After a few years, lifers become your better prisoners. They tend to adjust and just do their time. They tend to be a calming influence on the younger kids, and we have more problems with people serving shorter terms." It should also be noted that murderers are among those offenders least likely to repeat their crime even when released.[2]

State	Year	Support for Death Penalty	
		General Support	Beside Life Without Parole
California[3]	1989	79.5%	25.9%
Florida[4]	1986	84%	42%
Georgia#	1986	75%	46% 43%*
Idaho[5]	1990	79%	46%*
Kentucky[6]	1989	69.1%	35.9%
Massachusetts##	1990 NA	NA 30%*	.44%
Minnesota[7]	1992	67%	39.8%
Nebraska[8]	1991	80.4%	42.9% 26.1%*
New York[9]	1991	70.6%	35.8% 19.4%*
Oklahoma#	1988	80.2%	48%

* Life Without Parole Plus Restitution
# Figures reported in Kentucky and Nebraska studies.
Figures reported in New York study

Unpredictability of Future Violence

One important assumption in the argument for the death penalty as a means of preventing repeat offenses is that society's can make good predictions about the future violent acts of a defendant. A number of studies, however, have shown that society's predictions have usually not been accurate. In an unpublished study, James W. Marquart and Jonathan R. Sorensen traced the lives of 558 death row inmates whose executions were halted by the Furman versus Georgia decision in 1972. They found that four of the inmates committed murders in prison and one after he was released. In addition, they found that four of the inmates had been found to be innocent and released. Thus, less than one percent of the death row inmates murdered again. The authors stated that "executing all of them would not have greatly protected society. We would have executed nearly 600 inmates to protect us from five. And we would have killed four innocent people in the process."[10]

Marquart and Sorensen conducted a more in-depth study of 47 Texas inmates whose sentences were commuted due to the Furman decision. This study was conducted using a control group of 156 male inmates who had been sentenced to life imprisonment for murder (n=128) or rape (n=28). The groups were similar in age, race, violence of previous offenses, and length of imprisonment. In-prison behavior was measured by examining the prison records for each inmate.

It was found that 75 percent of former death row inmates committed no serious infractions, compared to 70 percent of the lifers who had committed no serious offenses. Ninety-three percent of the former death row inmates committed no offenses of the most violent kind (aggravated assault or fighting with a weapon), while 90 percent of the lifers committed none of these kinds of offenses. In other words, the former death row inmates had slightly better institutional records than did their counterparts in the control group. The researchers stated,

> The *Furman* inmates, as compared with the life sentence cohort, were not unusually disruptive or rebellious, nor did they pose a disproportionate threat to other inmates and staff, as had been

previously predicted by politicians, clinicians, and administrators.[11]

The study continued as inmates from both groups were released into the community. Sixty-six percent of the former death row inmates and 70 percent of the lifers were eventually returned to the community. As of the 1988 study date, 94 percent of the lifers and 86 percent of the former death row inmates had not been convicted of any new felonies. Unfortunately, one of the former death row inmates had committed another homicide and then committed suicide within a year of his release. None of the life convicts were known to have committed another murder.[12]

Marquart, Sorensen, and Sheldon Ekland-Olsen also conducted a study of the prison and community behavior of 90 inmates who had been sentenced to death but whose sentences were later commuted to life imprisonment. This study used three control groups: 107 inmates serving life sentences, all of the inmates in the Texas prison system, and the inmates serving in a single high security prison (the Darrington Unit). The results showed that the former death row inmates had a lower rate of violent offenses than all of the control groups. In yearly averages the former death row inmates had 1.61 violent infractions per 100 inmates compared to 2.60 for those under life sentence, 11.66 for the general population, and 19.54 for the Darrington unit.

In comparing the death sentence commutees with the lifers, the researches found that on January 1, 1989, about 90 percent of both groups were on trustee status. Two-thirds of both groups had never been in solitary confinement, a punishment for serious rules violations. Twenty-seven percent of the commuted group had no record of a rules violation compared to 22 percent of the control group.[13]

As with the post-Furman study, the researchers followed those commutees who were released into the community, along with members of the control group of inmates serving life sentences. Of the twelve former death row inmates who were released, only one had returned to prison. (The average release time in December 1988 was 4.5 years.) Of the thirteen who had been released from the control group, one had also been returned to prison, and he had been re-incarcerated several times.[14]

The results of these studies indicate that most convicts condemned to death can live out their lives in prison without repeating their murderous behavior. There are exceptions, but these are rare and difficult to predict. The sentence of life without parole, then, provides many inmates the possibility of rehabilitation at relatively little risk. The alternative is to kill inmates —a few of whom are genuinely dangerous, but most of whom pose relatively little risk to the lives of others, and some of whom are innocent. But executing inmates is always done at tremendous social and economic cost, as will be shown in later chapters of this book.

Conclusion

Life without parole is a viable alternative to the death penalty. As studies cited in this chapter have shown, society cannot know what the future holds for any human being. Most murderers, if given the chance, will live out their lives without killing again. Vicious murderers have at times been rehabilitated. Nor can society be certain its system of justice always operates correctly. In executing a criminal, the state can by no means be certain that it has not killed an innocent man.

In addition the process of carrying out an execution will prolong the suffering of victim families, through repeated hearings and through the efforts of death penalty opponents to humanize the offender.

Perhaps most importantly, however, in carrying out an execution, society has also given the message that lethal violence can be justified not just for self-defense but also for some imagined chance that someone might be dangerous in the future. Given the already violent nature of our society, it is doubtful that this is a good message for our government to be giving.

8
What About the Victims?

A powerful emotional argument for capital punishment is usually made by the family members of the victims. Death penalty opponents need to prepare themselves for facing the horrifying pain that these family members have experienced.

The fear and the terror that family members have faced is unimaginable. If the victim was missing for a period of time before the murder was discovered, the anxiety of not knowing what had happened was overwhelming. This was followed by the terrible discovery and perhaps a despairing disbelief. If the murder was particularly brutal—involving rape or torture—the family members had to face the fear and the pain their loved one experienced before death. This is especially difficult if the victim was a child.

Family members are likely to replay the last time they saw the loved one over and over again in their minds. They will wonder if there was anything they could have done to prevent the crime. They may feel guilt, even though there was nothing they could have done. They may also experience fear for other family members and for themselves.

Often they must deal with an insensitive police and legal system that has not kept them adequately informed. In some cases, they may have heard news of the case for the first time through the media, rather than personally from a police officer or district attorney. They feel powerless and forgotten.

If the families have other problems, their victimization may make them worse, as each family member works through pain and grief in different ways. Their preoccupation with the tragedy which has befallen them may eventually drive away some of their friends. So the original loss may be multiplied by other losses. In many cases, this pain and grief will turn into an awful anger—anger not just at the murderer but at the legal system and those who appear to take the murderer's side.

Compassion

Active opponents of the death penalty face the pain and grief of murder victims' families. Family members will speak for the death penalty in public forums, in legislative hearings, and perhaps even through individual telephone calls or confrontations. Sometimes they will express anger against opponents of capital punishment. When this occurs, death penalty opponents must be compassionate. They should never say or do anything to diminish the experience of these people. They must empathize and seek ways to help them.

The Death Penalty Is Hard on Victims' Families

One of the effects of capital punishment is to make the murderer rather than the victim the center of attention. Because the murderer is still alive, efforts will be made to save him. Attempts will be made to "humanize" him, to explain his behavior, to show him as a victim. Everything said about the murderer may be true, but it takes the focus away from the suffering experienced by the victim. Victims' families may rightly feel that their loved one is ignored in the process, and that they are forgotten while the murderer becomes the object of sympathy.

The legal process is also difficult for the families of victims. The trial and sentencing hearing are likely to bring out the most gruesome aspects of the crime. At each postconviction hearing, this information may be dredged up again. In addition, the long appeals procedure drags the whole process out. The families are not allowed to put the crime behind them but must periodically review it as each appeal hearing is held.

Life Without Parole and Victims' Families

One strength of a life without parole sentence is that it helps bring closure more quickly to the victim's family. Such a sentence usually presents fewer constitutional issues than a death sentence. The issues will also not be as pressing, and hearings and appeal attempts will be likely reduced.

The life-without-parole sentence also reduces the focus on the murderer. Placing a murderer in prison for life generates little chance that he will be the center of society's attention. Victims' families then can mourn their loss and move into the future without having to attend hearing after hearing in which a sympathetic view of the offender is presented.

The father of a murder victim in Colorado was relieved when his daughter's murderer received a life sentence rather than the death penalty. He stated, "It's final closure. I don't have to put my family or myself through this anymore."[1]

Finally, the amount of money used to carry out capital trials and appeals is very large. (See chapter thirteen for more detailed information on this issue.) If this money were not used for legal procedures surrounding the imposition of a death sentence, it could be made available for victims' families. Murder victims' families face many unexpected expenses. Funeral costs can be quite high, and many family members may require psychological counseling to cope with their loss. It can be argued that society would do more for these victims if it provided more financial support, instead of spending hundreds of thousands of dollars to execute the murderer.

Not All Murder Victims' Families Favor the Death Penalty

Although the anger of murder victims' families leads many family members to favor capital punishment, not all families that have experienced this kind of loss are death penalty proponents. The Kennedy family has lost two of its sons (John F. and Robert) to assassination but has remained opposed to capital punishment, as has the family of Martin Luther King Jr.

In addition to these more famous families, numerous other family members of victims oppose the death penalty. Bill

Pelke's grandmother was brutally stabbed to death by a gang of teenage girls. After a period of anger, he experienced a religious conversion in which he recognized that his anger was not who he wanted to be. He later befriended one of the girls, who was on Indiana's death row at the time. Since then he has spoken against the death penalty in United States and Italy.

Marietta Jaeger also has been an ardent spokeswoman against the death penalty. While on a family camping trip in Montana, her seven-year-old daughter was kidnaped and murdered.

Both Pelke and Jaeger have been active in Murder Victims Families for Reconciliation (MVFR), an organization for victim family members who oppose capital punishment. This organization has been one of the most active anti-death penalty groups in America. It has sponsored Journeys of Hope, multi-day marches against the death penalty. The first Journey was in Georgia in 1993. Later ones were in Indiana in 1994, California in 1995, and Virginia in 1996.[2] MVFR also has a newsletter, *The Voice*.

In the summer 1995 *Voice*, Kathy Dillon, whose father and boyfriend had been murdered at different times in her life, wrote,

> The pain, sadness, and trauma experienced by family and friends when a loved one is murdered is multiplied exponentially when a state-sponsored execution is carried out as a sentence for murder. The executed person leaves behind his or her loved ones, who must suffer this loss. I believe that no one, including the family of the condemned, should have to suffer such grief as that suffered when a loved one is intentionally killed. I believe that neither my father nor Dave would wish anyone the same pain that their families suffered when they were murdered.[3]

Statements such as Kathy Dillon's are a powerful witness against the death penalty. However, opponents of capital punishment must not use such statements to try to convince other murder victims' family members that they are somehow wrong or unforgiving if they are pro-capital punishment. These family members must be allowed to deal with their grief in whatever way may be best for them.

Rather than diminishing their grief, it is best simply to acknowledge their pain and to support programs for crime victims and their families as an alternative to spending money on capital punishment.

Conclusion

One of the most difficult and painful tasks death penalty opponents face is to respond to the calls for vengeance from the families of murder victims. This task should be performed with compassion and respect. Victims as well as murderers must be remembered in the work of those who oppose the death penalty.

Death penalty opponents should actively seek constructive ways to help murder victims' families. Advocating for victim-assistance programs is one way to do this. We should not be afraid to point out that the money spent in trying to kill the men and women on death row could be more effectively spent on such programs. It should be remembered that not all victims' families support the death penalty. Indeed, some of the most forceful and active opponents of capital punishment speak from this perspective.

9
The Death Penalty and Race

African-Americans Are Overrepresented on Death Row

Since the 1976 decision in Gregg versus Georgia which reinstated the United States death penalty, the death row population has consistently been about 40 percent African-American. African-Americans make up only about 12 percent of the American population. Death penalty proponents have argued that this discrepancy does not indicate judicial system racial prejudice. It simply points to the fact that African-American life is more violent and therefore produces more murderers who are ultimately sentenced to death.

The murder rate among African-Americans is much greater than the murder rate among white people.[1] But if we are to understand the discriminatory nature of the death penalty, we cannot stop there. We must ask *why* the murder rate among African-Americans is so much greater. African-Americans are not by nature more violent than white people. Studies by Brandon S. Centerwell have shown that rates of domestic homicide are not significantly different among African-Americans and whites in comparable socioeconomic circumstances.[2]

However, many African-Americans do not share the same socioeconomic status as most whites. Both past and present discrimination against African-Americans has left a huge socioeconomic gap between many African-Americans and the average white standard of living. In 1993, nearly one-third (31.3 percent) of black families lived below the poverty level. This compares to 9.4 percent of white families living in poverty.[3] In 1995, unemployment among African-Americans stood at 11.5 percent, more than double the 5.3 percent unemployment rate for whites. For young black men, unemployment was 37.6 percent.[4]

Because of poverty, African-Americans are more likely to live in overcrowded housing. They usually have poorer educational opportunities. They are more likely to live in neighborhoods infested with crime and substance abuse. Their young people have fewer recreational outlets. At their worst, these socioeconomic conditions lead many African-Americans to despair, hopelessness, and rage. And these in turn may lead to substance abuse, violence, and crime.

The greater murder rate among African-Americans, in other words, is attributable to the racial prejudice that causes this poverty. The death sentence is the result of some of these murders. Therefore, the disproportionate number of African-Americans on death row also can be attributed to racial discrimination.

In recent years, however, capital punishment proponents have pointed to statistics that show African-American murderers are less likely to draw a capital sentence than white murderers. For example, one study showed that blacks account for 48.5 percent of those arrested for homicide and nonnegligent manslaughter but make up only 40.9 percent of those on death row. Whites make up 50.2 percent of the adults arrested for murder and nonnegligent homicide, but 57.9 percent of those on death row. (These figures are from 1980 to 1984.)[5]

This seems a powerful argument against the claim of racial discrimination. In fact, however, it may point to another way in which capital punishment is discriminatory.

The Race-of-Victim Issue

Many social scientists believe that the most important reason African-American murderers are less likely to receive the death penalty is that typically their victims are also African-Americans. Between 1976 and 1993, only about 51 percent of all homicide victims were white.[6] In those murders for which defendants have been executed since the reinstatement of the death penalty, however, nearly 83 percent of the victims were white.[7] On the other hand, about 46 percent of the homicide victims between 1976 and 1993 were African-American, but only 12 percent of those offenders who were executed received the death sentence for killing a black.

In 1994, then, 94 percent of African-American murder victims were killed by black offenders, whereas 84 percent of white victims were killed by whites.[8] This figure is consistent with figures for the previous ten years. Although black murderers kill six times more African-American than they do whites, they are twice as likely to be executed for killing a white person as for killing someone of their own race.[9] Through April 1995, then, 94 black defendants had been executed for killing whites compared to only 43 for killing other African-Americans.

Statistics such as these have led death penalty opponents to look at the race of the victim as one of the determinants for whether or not the defendant would receive the death penalty. In the 1987 case of McCleskey versus Kemp, a study made by David Baldus of the University of Iowa showed the following pattern:[10]

Race of Defendant/ Race of Victim	Number Receiving Death Penalty	Percent Receiving Death Penalty
Black/White	50 of 223	22%
White/White	8 of 748	8%
Black/Black	18 of 1443	1%
White/Black	2 of 60	3%

Using statistical analysis of these figures and other variables, Baldus concluded there was a pattern of discrimination based on the race of the victim. The Baldus study was immediately attacked by the U.S. Department of Justice and others who supported capital punishment, but a number of leading statisticians and criminologists were moved to file a brief with the U.S. Supreme Court in support of the study and Baldus's conclusions. They stated,

Statistical evidence *can* determine with great reliability whether racial factors are playing a role in the sentencing system as a whole and whether the disparities are so great as to tip the balance of probability that they operated in any particular case. Baldus's studies provide just such evidence.[11]

Testifying before Congress, Baldus cited studies in a number of different states showing that murderers of whites were more likely to face the death penalty than murderers of African-Americans. He used this table to show how much more likely the murderer of a white person was to receive a death sentence compared to a murderer of an African-American:

State	Death Odds Multiplier
Arkansas	3.6
Florida	4.8
Georgia	7.2
Illinois	4.0
Mississippi	5.5
North Carolina	4.4
Oklahoma	4.3

In other words, the murderer of a white person in Arkansas is 3.6 times more likely to receive the death penalty than the murderer of an African-American. Baldus postulated a number of reasons for this discriminatory pattern of sentencing. He noted that he and other researchers felt that

the racial disparities . . . flow principally from prosecutorial decisions whether to charge defendants with capital crimes, whether to allow defendants in death-eligible cases to plead guilty to noncapital offenses, and, in cases in which the prosecutor has secured a conviction for a capital offense, whether to waive unilaterally the death penalty.

Baldus went on to state what he thought to be the reasons for these differences in the behavior of prosecutors. He mentioned the greater publicity typically brought on by the murder of a white person and greater public pressure for punitive action against the perpetrator. He also pointed to the greater influence that the families of white victims were likely to have with prosecutors, most of whom are white and therefore can more easily identify with the families of a white victim. Last, he mentioned that a capital trial might not seem worth the heavy costs for the murder of an African-American victim who has had little visibility or influence in the community.[12]

While Baldus's conclusions continue to be disputed by the proponents of capital punishment, few would deny that racial discrimination exists in our society and can influence the judicial system that condemns men and women to death. The following exchange occurred between Representative John Conyers, a member of the Congressional black caucus, and Assistant Attorney General Edward Dennis, who was testifying against the Racial Justice Act of 1990, which would have outlawed capital punishment in cases where a racially discriminatory pattern could be shown. (The act was not passed.)

Conyers:	Do you believe that race is a factor in criminal justice in America?
Dennis:	Yes, I do.
Conyers:	All right. Do you believe race is a factor, then, in capital cases?
Dennis:	Yes.
Conyers:	Well, then, if you were a lawyer for a person, an African-American, who is facing the death sentence, and you were asked by him what the likelihood of receiving the death sentence, would you tell him that the most significant fact in the case could be that the victim was white?
Dennis:	I don't think I can answer that in a hypothetical way. I don't believe as a general proposition that—well, let me put it this way: I think that I would certainly have to take into account the possibility that members of the jury or the prosecution might be swayed to view the crime as being more serious, perhaps, if there was some racial aspect to it.[13]

Finally, we have the words of the United States Supreme Court itself in upholding the death penalty in the McCleskey decision. The court stated that racial disparities were "an inevitable part of our criminal justice system." In other cases, perhaps such disparities, no matter how unfortunate, must be accepted until society itself changes; but in capital cases, such disparities will cost people their lives.

Conclusion

Capital punishment applied in a way known to be discriminatory is the ultimate act of injustice. In America, a disproportionate number of African-Americans are placed on death row. This disproportionate number is one result of the racism that infects our country to such an extent that it has been called "the original sin of America." The fact that the murder of a white victim is much more likely to draw a death sentence than the murder of a black victim also shows that in America, African-Americans are less valued than whites, even to the point of death. If we cannot eliminate such racial injustice, then we should at least not allow it to follow its natural course to the final and fatal conclusion of the death penalty.

10
The Death Penalty and the Mentally Retarded

Mental retardation is defined as "significantly subaverage general intellectual functioning existing concurrently with deficits in adaptive behavior and manifested during the developmental period."[1]

The mentally retarded make up about 3 percent of the total population in the United States. They make up about 10 percent of the men and women on death row.[2] Many people are surprised that any mentally retarded people are on death row at all, let alone that they would be overrepresented. Over the years, it has been shown that the mentally retarded are less likely to be violent than people whose intelligence level is within the normal range.[3] Why, then, do so many mentally retarded defendants receive the death penalty?

Traits of Mental Retardation

Basically, mentally retarded defendants are more likely to receive the death penalty because they are easier to convict. Mental retardation has a number of characteristics that make a mentally retarded person particularly susceptible to aggressive police and prosecution tactics that can create a strong case against the person even when innocent.

A major article on the mentally retarded in the criminal justice system by James W. Ellis (who later became president of the American Association on Mental Retardation) and Ruth. W. Luckasson lists six characteristics of mentally retarded people that would affect their ability to function adequately within the criminal justice system. These include communication and memory problems, impulsivity, limited moral development, lack of knowledge, denial of disability, and motivational differences. Each characteristic can cause the individual problems as she or he is going through the process of arrest and trial.[4]

Retarded individuals may not be able to adequately communicate in a high-stress situation, such as arrest or the witness stand. At such times they are likely to look to others for leadership. On the other hand, they may be unresponsive to police officers because they don't know what to say. They may refuse to answer questions which are beyond their ability to comprehend. Their limited memory may make it difficult to assist an attorney in presenting a defense. Memory and communication problems can also make their testimony appear suspect, since they may not be able to remember details of the situation or they may appear to be confused on the witness stand.

Mentally retarded individuals are less able to resist impulsive urges. They may accompany others on impulse or commit crimes on impulse. This impulsivity may also make it difficult for mentally retarded persons to control inappropriate sexual behavior, which may be linked to being sexually victimized themselves or to institutionalized training that has traditionally repressed normal sexual feelings.[5] In addition, their impulsivity also makes it difficult for them to focus on pertinent facts or events when they are being questioned about their case. Again, this limits their ability to assist in their own defense.

Limited moral development makes the mentally retarded tend to look at events in black-and-white terms. If something bad has happened, there must be someone to blame. If there is no one else, they may accept the blame themselves. As Ellis and Luckasson state,

> A defendant with retardation may plead guilty to a crime which he did not commit because he believes the blame should be assigned to someone. . . . Similarly, some people with mental retardation will eagerly assume blame to please or curry favor with an accuser.[6]

Because mental retardation is stigmatized in our society, mentally retarded individuals often work hard to deny their disability. They do their best to hide the fact that they do not understand everything going on around them. Many mentally retarded people who are operating on a higher functional level have the ability to conceal their retardation.

In attempting to disguise their disability, however, they may take responsibility for an act that they consider to be clever in order to cover up their retardation. A mentally retarded defendant, for example, may brag about "outsmarting" a victim. A mentally retarded defendant may also behave in an inappropriate manner during the trial. If a "street kid," he or she may continue to behave in a manner more fit for the street than for the courtroom.

Patricia Smith represented Jerome Bowden, a mentally retarded man who was executed in Georgia in 1986. She was also president of the Association for Retarded Citizens in Georgia. After Bowden's execution, she stated in an editorial,

> The significant variable is that people with mental retardation are much less likely to learn the values of society by osmosis than are persons with a higher IQ. A kid with mental retardation who grows up on the streets probably has little or no exposure to the values the larger society calls "right and wrong." Bowden only knew what he experienced and he only experienced the streets.[7]

Mentally retarded people also lack knowledge. They may not know their basic rights and thus are likely to give up their rights upon arrest. They may not know they should ask for an attorney or how to do so.

Mentally retarded people are motivated by praise of people that they perceive to be in authority. They will try their best to please those who they think have authority. As Ellis and Luckasson state, "The desire to please authority figures does appear to be a powerful motivator." This seems to be especially true if the mentally retarded person has ever been institutionalized.

Thus police officers can convince mentally retarded persons that if they confess to the crime, everything will turn out right. In the case of Jerome Bowden, a detective told him, "If you'll sign this, I'll try to help you." Bowden signed a prepared confession—a confession he could not read.[8]

These traits of mental retardation not only make it easier for the police and prosecutors to convict a mentally retarded person. They also make it easier for other criminals to turn a mentally retarded accomplice into a "fall guy" for a crime. Criminals may convince mentally retarded persons to confess, even to a crime they did not commit.

Recognizing their own vulnerability, nonretarded co-defendants may plea-bargain in exchange for their testimony against the retarded individual. Mentally retarded people will be less likely to do this, since their moral development may lead them to value loyalty to a friend over self-preservation. In addition, their inability to provide convincing testimony may lead to the police being less willing to make a deal with them if they do offer to testify against a codefendant.

The Beginnings of Abolition

In 1989, the United States Supreme Court in the case of Penry versus Lynaugh decided that mental retardation must be considered in sentencing, but that it was not unconstitutional to execute a mentally retarded person. At the same time, the Court seemed to indicate that if enough state legislatures enacted statutes exempting mentally retarded defendants from possible execution, they might revisit the issue.

Many have recognized the injustice of executing adults whose intellectual capacities resemble those of a child of twelve or less. This has led to efforts in a number of states to pass laws exempting the mentally retarded from capital punishment. By the middle of 1995, Arkansas, Colorado, Georgia, Indiana, Kentucky, Maryland, New Mexico, Tennessee, and Washington had passed such legislation. The legislation in these states, along with the twelve states that do not practice capital punishment, means that 42 percent of the states no longer allow a person known to be mentally retarded to be executed.

In addition, a number of state polls have shown that the majority of citizens oppose using the death penalty on the mentally retarded. Some of these results are as follows:

State	Year	Support for Death Penalty	
		In General	For the Retarded
California[9]	1989	79.5%	26%
Florida[10]	1986	84%	12%
Georgia#	1986	75%	33%
Kentucky[11]	1989	69.1%	15%
Maryland#	NA	64%	46%
New York[12]	1991	70.6%	10%
Oklahoma#	1988	80.2%	29%
National[13]	1995	78%	9%

#Cited in California poll results.

Because of the emotional aspects of executing mentally retarded men and women, the issue of capital punishment for mentally retarded offenders is one that abolitionists have used as a beginning point. Even winning this point in the current punitive environment is not easy, however. Retentionists recognize that this is a "foot in the door" approach and are likely to fight it.

Conclusion

Still, as James Ellis pointed out in his testimony before the Senate Judiciary Committee, only one percent of homicides actually receive a death sentence. He added,

To permit the execution of a person with mental retardation requires concluding that such an individual is both in the bottom two percent of the population in intelligence and also in the top one percent of the population in his appreciation and understanding of the wrongfulness of his actions. *We strongly believe that, as a practical matter, no one can be in both categories.* We therefore believe that sentencing any person with mental retardation to death represents a tragic injustice.[14]

11
Capital Punishment— for People with No Capital

The race and mental ability of defendants will probably be important in determining whether they will receive the death penalty. However, the key factor appears to be whether or not defendants can afford to hire a competent attorney.

About 90 percent of death row inmates could not afford their own attorney for their initial trial.[1] In 1989, there were 226 persons on California's death row. Of these, only two (less than one percent of the total number) could afford their own attorney for the appeals process.[2] Thus it may be that African-Americans and mentally retarded defendants are overrepresented on death row partly because these two groups also tend to be poor.

Differences for Poor and Affluent Defendants

The difference between those who can afford an attorney and those who cannot begins at the time of arrest and becomes more evident throughout the trial process. For example, when an affluent person is arrested, he may already have a family attorney who can step in immediately. Affluent defendants will normally have a better education and be better informed of their right to an attorney. They are more likely to have a support system of friends and family who can exert influence on their behalf at the time of arrest.

If defendants are poor and uneducated, they may not fully understand their right to an attorney even when given a Miranda warning. If they do ask for an attorney, they will have to wait for one to be appointed. In the meantime, they will have to wait in jail. This can lead them to feel pressured to talk to the police without their attorney present, in hopes they can prove their innocence or explain away their offense.

It is also likely that the police will treat an affluent defendant differently than a poor defendant. If aware that a person has influential friends, police are less likely to use pressure techniques. They may also be careful if they know a private attorney will be hired who will have time to look more closely at police conduct during the case.

The attorney appointed for the poor person will be a public defender. Most public defenders are hard working and competent attorneys but have many cases and may give less attention to the case than an attorney paid by an individual or his family. Public defenders often have less experience. This job is frequently taken by attorneys who have recently graduated from law school. In Idaho, for example, Donald Paradis, a capital defendant condemned to death, was represented by an attorney who had been out of law school for less than a year.

In addition, not all public defenders are good lawyers. Public defenders are sometimes sought on a bid basis, and the attorneys hired are the low bidders. This may mean that they lack the experience or competence to maintain a private practice without seeking relatively low-paying contract work. They may also see their contract work as less important than cases likely to bring in more money.

Stephen B. Bright, in an article for the *Yale Law Journal*, cited numerous examples of how overworked or incompetent public defenders failed to adequately defend capital cases or to present mitigating circumstances during the sentencing phase of the trials. Included in this number are cases where defense attorneys slept through parts of the trial or were drunk or under the influence of drugs in court. Some of these cases ultimately led to executions of the defendants.[3]

Prosecutors will be influenced by the defense attorney. Strong defense attorneys are more likely to be able to plead down the charge, since it is much more likely they can win the case outright. Prosecutors may also prefer to work on a lesser charge simply to avoid the numerous delays a good defense attorney can create.

Prosecutors may also see the affluent defendant as someone with potential for rehabilitation. The affluent defendant will normally be better educated, more articulate, and often appear to have a better social support system. The middle-class prosecutor may feel more at home with such defendants and thus be more sympathetic to them. For an affluent defendant, then, a capital charge may never be considered even though the crime is equal in gravity to the crime of a poor defendant who is charged with capital crime. In the O. J. Simpson case, for example, it was announced long before the criminal trial that the prosecutors would not seek the death penalty, even though the case involved a heinous double murder.

If a capital charge is brought against a person with money, the defendant will have the advantage of having a complete law office working on his case. The attorney will be able to use the time of law clerks to do the legal searching for precedents and other legal loopholes. Clerical help will write letters, prepare reports, and do the paperwork involved in trying a case. Public defenders, who normally work under strict expense limitations, will probably have to do most of their own legal research, taking away time from investigating the actual case.[4] They will have less access to clerical assistance. The private attorney will also be able to pay for private investigators to look for witnesses and other evidence. The poor defendant will usually not have access to the same quality of investigatory help.

Finally, even if an affluent defendant is convicted, the judge who decides the sentence will see the defendant as someone much like himself or herself. Like the prosecutor, the judge may see a greater chance of rehabilitation for the middle-class defendant, with whom he identifies.

Thus the poor are much more likely to receive the death penalty than affluent defendants who have committed the same crime. In America, this has been widely accepted. A 1991 Gallup poll found that 60 percent of those questioned believed poor people more likely to receive the death penalty for the same crime than people of average or above average income.[5]

As Justice William O. Douglas commented in his response to the Furman case, "One searches our chronicles in vain for the execution of any member of the affluent strata in this society."[6]

Conclusion

The outcome of a potential capital case in our criminal justice system largely depends on how much money the defendant has. It is human nature for people who are more powerful to receive better treatment in all aspects of life. In the case of capital punishment, however, this difference is a matter of life and death. In the United States, people receive the death sentence because they are poor, not simply because of the crime they committed. A wealthy defendant will not die for the same crime for which a poor defendant will receive a death sentence. The question we must ask this: Do we want a society that kills people because they are poor?

12
The Innocent Have Been Executed

The strongest single argument against the death penalty is that innocent people might be executed. We think with horror of what it is like for a person to await execution, knowing he is innocent. We also know that if we make a mistake in a capital case, there will be no chance to make it right. The innocent person is dead. There is no way to bring him back. As a society, we will have to live with that guilt and will have no way of making restitution.

The argument is also powerful because it puts us in danger. If innocent people can be executed, we too could be executed for being in the wrong place at the wrong time. These emotions make execution of the innocent one of the death penalty abolitionists' most powerful arguments.

The best source of information about people who were innocent but condemned to death is *In Spite of Innocence.*[1] This book lists 416 twentieth-century cases in which people were accused of capital crimes and yet later proved to be innocent. In most cases, the accused were convicted and given a death sentence. Twenty-three of the cases resulted in wrongful executions. An additional twenty-seven resulted in executions stayed within three days of the execution date.

The authors have estimated that their numbers on all counts are low—and that they are particularly low when it comes to those who were actually executed. After a person has been put to death, the prosecution is not likely to reopen the case. Defense attorneys and investigators must move on to new cases to avert other executions. Witnesses are not likely to change their testimony nor new witnesses to come forward. Thus the number of wrongful executions is probably considerably higher than twenty-three.

The authors of *In Spite of Innocence* have listed four reasons for wrongful convictions in capital cases: false information given by witnesses, prejudice against defendants, faulty police work, and overzealous prosecution. Below are some examples of each kind of wrongful capital conviction. Unless otherwise stated, these cases are explored by *In Spite of Innocence*.

False Information from Witnesses

The first reason for wrongful convictions is wrong information given by witnesses. Witnesses may simply be mistaken. An example of mistaken information occurred in the case of Timothy Hennis, a U.S. Army sergeant convicted of murder and sentenced to death in South Carolina in 1986. One witness said he had seen Hennis at the site of the murder. At retrial, the defense was able to produce a neighbor of the victim who looked like Hennis. Another witness said she had seen Hennis use the victim's bank card at an automatic teller. Later, it was shown that she could not have been at the bank at the same time the card was used. Hennis was acquitted.

The second kind of false information is given by witnesses who lie to assure the defendant is convicted. This may happen because the real killer is attempting to shift blame to someone else. Thus in a famous case, Randall Adams was convicted of the 1976 killing of a Dallas (Texas) police officer chiefly on evidence given by David Ray Harris. Adams's story was featured in the film *The Thin Blue Line*, which detailed the many inconsistencies in Harris's story. Adams was released in 1989. It is now generally believed that Harris was the actual murderer.

At other times, defendants may be falsely accused by someone with a grudge. In 1974 Joseph Brown was convicted of murder and sentenced to death, based on the evidence of Ronald Floyd. Floyd had been angered by Brown's confession to a robbery that implicated Floyd as an accomplice. Floyd later retracted his testimony, but in the meantime Brown had come within thirteen hours of execution. He was released in 1987.

The problem of witnesses is an important one in capital cases. Often in such cases, one defendant has been convicted on the word of another person also involved in the crime. Frequently the charge against the accomplice is plea-bargained down to bring about cooperation. In many cases, however, it is difficult to tell who was the murderer and who was the accomplice. This decision is often based on who can tell the most convincing story to police or even on who makes a deal first.

An example occurred in 1983, when Anthony Brown was sentenced to death for murder in Florida, based on the evidence given by a codefendant who received life imprisonment. The conviction was appealed. At a retrial in 1986, the codefendant admitted lying at the first trial. Brown was released after serving three years on death row.

Prejudice Against the Defendant

A second reason for wrongful convictions is prejudice against the defendant. In chapters nine, ten, and eleven, we have shown the problems created by racial discrimination, mental retardation, and poverty in capital cases. All could influence the way a judge and jury will relate to a defendant. The same can be true if the defendant exhibits other "undesirable" traits. For example, a defendant may be tainted if he is a homosexual or if he belongs to an undesirable group, such as a motorcycle gang.

In 1974 a group of five motorcyclists were accused of the mutilation murder of a young homosexual in Albuquerque, New Mexico. The fear of violent motorcycle gangs became an important issue in the trial. Based on the inconsistent evidence of one witness, and ignoring strong proof of an alibi, the jury convicted four of the motorcyclists. They were sentenced to death. Only when Kerry Lee, a drifter, confessed to the crime to South Carolina authorities in 1975 were charges dropped and the four falsely accused men released.

There is also the case of Clarence Brandley, a black school

janitor convicted in 1981 and sentenced to death for the rape and murder of a young white high school girl in Conroe, Texas.[2] When Brandley was first questioned about the murder, he was told by a police officer someone would have to "hang" for the murder, and "Since you're the nigger, you're elected." During one hearing, a woman was heard chanting, "Kill that nigger, kill that nigger!" A jury member who held out against the conviction during Brandley's first trial was accused of being a "nigger lover." The case is a continuing story of shoddy investigation, perjury, and prosecutorial and judicial misconduct. The judge's secretary said that during the time of the trial, working in the judge's office "was like working on a project to convict Clarence Brandley." After the trial important evidence disappeared.

At an evidentiary hearing held in 1987, Appeals Judge Perry Pickett stated about this case,

> For the past ten days, I have presided over the evidentiary hearing to try to determine if equal justice under the law has been self-evident from all of the evidence adduced under oath. The litany of events graphically described by the witnesses, some of it chilling and shocking, leads me to the conclusion [that] the pervasive shadow of darkness has obscured the light of fundamental decency and human rights. . . . [The investigative procedure was] so impermissibly suggestive that false testimony was created, thereby denying . . . due process of law and a fundamentally fair trial. . . . [The State] had wholly ignored any evidence or leads to evidence that might prove inconsistent with their premature conclusion that Brandley had committed the murder. The conclusion is inescapable that the investigation was not conducted to solve the crime, but to convict Brandley.

Clarence Brandley was finally released in 1990, but as Jim McCloskey, an investigator who worked on the case, stated,

> Clarence Brandley is lucky. He is lucky because his case developed a lot of notoriety. A lot of good and competent people came to his aid—the public, lawyers, and investigators. He's lucky because there are a lot of Clarence Brandleys, and they are still buried in prison or on death row.

Two of the most famous twentieth-century capital trials also resulted in executions influenced more by political prejudice than by any substantial evidence. Joe Hill, an organizer for the International Workers of the World—the Wobblies—was tried, convicted, and executed in Utah in 1915, based on the weakest circumstantial evidence. The trial appeared to be more about Hill's union activities than about the murders of which he was accused.

Similarly, Nicola Sacco and Bartolomeo Vanzetti were executed in Massachusetts in 1927 for a murder committed in 1920. Admitted anarchists, Sacco and Vanzetti were tried in the days of the Red Scare which immediately followed the Russian Revolution. At one time, the judge in the case commented to friends, "Did you see what I did to those anarchist bastards the other day? I guess that will hold them for awhile."

We might like to believe that such blatantly political cases have not occurred in the past few years. However, at least one current capital case has troubling political overtones. Mumia Abu-Jamal was a well-known African-American journalist in Philadelphia. He had angered the city police by helping to begin the Black Panther chapter when he was a teenager. Later he had been critical of the police when they had bombed the home of MOVE, a black anarchist organization.

In 1981 Mumia Abu-Jamal was accused of murdering Daniel Faulkner, a Philadelphia police officer. Abu-Jamal had been found critically wounded near Faulkner's body but claimed he had been shot by Faulkner. Then Faulkner had been shot by an unknown assailant. The police produced two witnesses who said Abu-Jamal was the killer. However, one witness was a prostitute who later had drug charges against her dropped. The other was a cab driver whose testimony changed from that given on the night of the murder. Four other witnesses claimed they had seen another black man run from the scene. Since the original trial, another witness has come forward with a similar story.

The police also reported that Abu-Jamal had confessed to the crime after he had been taken to the hospital, but the prosecution did not reveal the confession until two months later. Nor was the confession included in the police report, and one police report made at the time recorded that Abu-Jamal had made no statement. There were also important discrepancies in the physical evidence. Faulkner was killed with a .44 caliber pistol; Mumia carried a .38. The police did not test Mumia's weapon to see if it had been recently fired.

At the trial, Abu-Jamal's political beliefs were the core of the prosecution's argument for the death penalty. Indeed Abu-Jamal in almost any circumstances would not be considered a capital defendant. He has no prior record. Premeditation was not proved.[3]

At the time of this writing, the facts of the case remain uncertain and hotly debated. But certainly there are questions about how the case was originally investigated and tried. Was perjury suborned to remove an enemy of the police? Was a confession falsified? Why was the prosecution allowed to bring Abu-Jamal's political beliefs into the argument for the death penalty? Why was this a capital case to begin with? These questions have led many to believe that the death sentence imposed had more to do with Abu-Jamal's political views rather than with the crime. An international effort to save Abu-Jamal has been launched.

Faulty Police Work

When a capital crime occurs, the police are often placed under tremendous pressure to find the criminal as quickly as possible. People are frightened; they feel unsafe. The police feel they need to find the killer quickly or there will be political consequences.

Working under this kind of pressure, the police often make mistakes. They may jump to conclusions too quickly. Then their work is no longer to find the killer but to validate the theory they have created about the crime.

Under these circumstances, the police may overlook evidence that does not meet their needs. In the worst cases, they may even withhold such evidence from the defense. They may also give too much significance to other evidence, such as statements from people whose credibility is weak. They may pressure witnesses to provide the best possible story for the prosecution, rather than looking for testimony to find out what really happened. They may also use pressure tactics to force a defendant to confess.

An example occurred in 1975. Johnny Ross, an African-American teenager, age sixteen, was convicted of rape of a white woman and was sentenced to death. The sentence was the result of dubious eyewitness testimony and a confession Ross claimed he made only after he was beaten by the police. The sentence was vacated by the Federal Courts for statutory reasons, but the conviction was upheld on appeal. In 1980 it was found that the blood type of the sperm found in the victim did not match Ross's blood type. He was released in 1981.

In another case William Jent and Earnest Miller were convicted of rape and murder in Florida in 1980. In 1986 the identity of the victim was established. Reexamination of the autopsy report revealed that the murder could not have been conducted in the way described by the witnesses. The report also gave a time of death for which Jent and Miller had an alibi. In 1983 the two men had been within sixteen hours of execution, but they were released in 1988. In 1991 they were awarded $65,000 from the Pasco County Sheriff Department because of its mishandling of the case.

Overzealous Prosecution

Like the police, prosecutors are under pressure to achieve convictions in death penalty cases. Often elected on "get tough on crime" platforms, prosecutors have placed themselves in the position of having to get convictions no matter what the cost. This can result in trying cases for which there is little evidence.

For example, Anibal Jaramillo was convicted of murder in Florida in 1981. He was sentenced to death, based on the evidence of one witness. However, this witness also claimed to have seen another man at the scene of the crime. There was also a couple who placed a second man at the scene of the murder. The prosecutor had no explanation for this second man. On appeal, Jaramillo's conviction was overturned because the evidence was "not legally sufficient to establish a *prima facie* case."

In a 1975 Arizona case, Jonathan Treadaway was convicted and sentenced to death for a "murder" that may not have been a murder. Treadaway was accused of sodomizing and murdering a six-year-old boy. At his retrial, however, a panel of pathologists testified that they believed the boy had died of pneumonia, and that there was no evidence of sodomy. The jury also reported that the prosecutor had failed to prove that Treadaway had ever been in the victim's home.

A Wrongful Execution

With the exception of the cases of Joe Hill and Sacco and Vanzetti, the cases cited above are all from the post-Furman era. Since that case, the legal system has theoretically provided safeguards to prevent the arbitrary and capricious use of the death sentence. In each of the cases above, except the still-pending Abu-Jamal case, the wrongful conviction was overturned. Sadly, this has not always been true. In the case of James Adams, it appears that an innocent man was executed.

Adams went to Florida's electric chair for the 1974 murder of Edgar Brown, a white former deputy sheriff. Adams was African-American, a prison escapee serving time for a rape. His rape conviction was based solely on the word of a white woman in Tennessee. There had been no physical evidence of the rape, and Adams claimed that he was innocent. However, the rape conviction was used against him at his trial for murder.

At the trial one eyewitness described the killer as a man with a darker complexion than Adams and as a man who had no moustache. Adams wore a moustache. This witness failed to pick out Adams in a police lineup and gave unconvincing testimony at the trial. Another witness who placed Adams at the scene was angry at Adams because he thought Adams was having an affair with his wife. This witness was later given a lie detector test which showed that it was questionable whether he had told the truth at the trial.

Adams claimed he had lent his car to a young woman at the time of the murder. This woman was heavyset and from a distance could easily have been mistaken for a man. Her pretrial deposition gave Adams an alibi, but she changed her testimony at the trial. She was not challenged by Adams's attorney.

A report on hair taken from the victim's hand as he was being taken to the hospital—hair presumably of his attacker—was not presented until three days after Adams was convicted. Even then this evidence was not given to Adams's attorneys.

Despite these many inconsistencies, the Adams conviction moved through the appeals process without being overturned. On May 10, 1984, James Adams went to Florida's electric chair.

It should be clear from the stories outlined above that innocent men and women are convicted in capital cases. Sometimes they are executed. The post-Furman protections have not kept these convictions from occurring. Indeed, the authors of *In Spite of Innocence* have identified at least thirty-one innocent men who have been sentenced to death since the Furman decision. The chart on the next page lists the names of these men, the year of their conviction, the state where convicted, and the date of the final disposition of their case, if given.

The Herrera Case

In view of the frequency with which innocent men and women are convicted of capital crimes, we expect that the judicial system would desire to maintain every possible safeguard against a possible wrongful execution. However, in the 1993 case of Herrera versus Collins, the United States Supreme Court held that Federal courts should not consider new evidence of innocence unless it was the result of procedural error on the part of state courts.

Leonel Herrera was convicted of killing two Texas police officers in 1981. Herrera had confessed to killing one of the officers. For this he received a life sentence. He was tried for the murder of the other policeman and received the death penalty. After the death of Herrera's brother Raul, members of his family claimed Raul, not Leonel, had actually murdered the policemen. These family members took lie detector tests which supported their version of events.

Year	Innocent Person	State	Race	Disposition
1973	James Creamer	Georgia	White	1975
1974	Joseph Brown	Florida	Black	1987
1974	Richard Greer	New Mexico	White	1975
1974	Thomas Gladish	New Mexico	White	1975
1974	Ronald Keine	New Mexico	White	1975
1974	Clarence Smith	New Mexico	White	1975
1974	James Adams	Florida	Black	Executed 1984
1974	Delbert Tibbs	Florida	Black	1982
1975	Johnny Ross	Louisiana	Black	1981
1975	Jonathan Treadaway	Arizona	White	Not given
1975	Jerry Banks	Georgia	Black	1980
1975	Earl Charles	Georgia	Black	1978
1977	Randall Adams	Texas	White	1989
1977	Henry Drake	Georgia	White	1987
1978	Larry Hicks	Indiana	Black	1980
1978	Anthony Peek	Florida	Black	1987
1978	Charles Giddens	Oklahoma	Black	1981
1979	Darby Williams	Illinois	Black	1987
1979	Perry Cobb	Illinois	Black	1987
1980	Earnest Miller	Florida	White	1988
1980	Jerry Bigelow	California	White	1988
1980	William Jent	Florida	White	1988
1981	Clarence Brandley	Texas	Black	1990
1981	Anibal Jaramillo	Florida	Hispanic	Not given
1982	Neil Ferber	Pennsylvania	White	1986
1983	Larry Troy	Florida	Black	1987
1983	Anthony Brown	Florida	Black	1986
1983	Willie Brown	Florida	Black	1987
1983	Juan Ramos	Florida	Hispanic	1987
1986	Timothy Hennis	North Carolina	White	1989
1988	Bradley Scott	Florida	White	1991

However, the Texas statute does not allow the introduction of new evidence unless presented in the thirty-day period specified by the law. The majority decision of the United States Supreme Court was that the Court should not interfere with this or similar statutes. The executive branch of the state government was the place to deal with actual innocence, after the initial trial and the statutory time limits on appeals.

Opponents of the death penalty, however, felt that this decision could lead to more executions of innocent people. In a dissenting opinion, Justice Harry A. Blackmun stated, "The execution of a person who can show he is innocent comes perilously close to simple murder."

Opponents of the death penalty also pointed out that many governors and other elected officials have often been elected to office based on an anticrime platform that includes support for the death penalty.[4] This may create political pressure that makes them unwilling to stop executions, even if there is strong evidence of innocence.

In the Herrera case, the executive branch refused to step in. Despite evidence that seemed at least to raise reasonable doubt about his guilt, Texas Governor Ann Richardson refused his request for a reprieve. Herrera was executed by lethal injection on May 12, 1993.

The Case of Jesse Jacobs

Another recent case of the execution of a potentially innocent man was that of Jesse Jacobs, executed on January 4, 1995.[5] Jacobs was tried and convicted as the "triggerman" in the murder of a woman who was having a conflict with his sister. Jacobs confessed to the murder but later retracted his confession, claiming his sister had killed the woman. He had only taken his sister to the woman's house. He claimed he had not known his sister was going to kill the woman. Still, he was tried, found guilty, and sentenced to death.

Later, the same prosecutor who had tried Jacobs prosecuted his sister. This time, the prosecutor claimed that the *sister* had actually killed the woman. At the trial, he stated,

I'm convinced that [Jacob's sister] is the one who pulled the trigger. And I'm convinced that Jesse Jacobs is telling the truth when he says that [his sister] pulled the trigger.

Legally, Jacobs could be executed as a non-triggerman, but this would require that the prosecution show Jacobs instigated the crime and either paid or coerced the actual killer. Since the prosecutor at his trial claimed Jacob's had actually killed the woman, however, it would be impossible for the prosecution to have proved that Jacobs influenced someone else to kill the victim. At the least, Jacobs deserved a new trial.

Echoing Justice Harry Blackmun's opinion in Herrera versus Collins, Jesse Jacobs stated on the night of his execution, "I have news for all of you. This is not going to be an execution. This is premeditated murder by the state of Texas."

Conclusion

The possibility of executing the innocent is the ghost that lurks behind the gallows. It is a powerful argument against even the most stout defenders of the death penalty. This ghost haunts public opinion and is one of the reasons, along with the human aversion to murder, that polls on capital punishment are so contradictory and fluid.

The fact that innocent men and women are convicted of capital offenses should argue against the current trend of reducing the number of avenues of appeal in capital cases. The public needs to be reminded that if a mistake is made in a capital case, there will be no way to make restitution. Instead, our society risks being as guilty of premeditated and unwarranted murder as any man or woman on death row.

13
The Cost of Death

It is a common misconception that the use of the death penalty saves money. People assume that killing an inmate is cheaper than keeping him in prison for the rest of his life.

Under the current system, however, this is not true. A 1988 study of death penalty costs in Florida showed that each execution cost $3.2 million dollars, compared to $516,000 for keeping the person in prison for 40 years. In Texas, a study made in 1992 estimated that each execution cost $2.3 million, three times the cost of keeping a person in maximum security for 40 years. Californians were told in 1988 that eliminating capital punishment could save $90 million annually.[1]

Process Costs

Costs of capital punishment come largely from the increased expenses of capital trials and appeals. Because a mistake in a death penalty trial could cost an innocent person his life, extraordinary procedures are used to try to assure fairness. Since most of the defendants in capital cases are indigent, the government will typically have to pay the costs of both the prosecution and the defense, along with all the court costs. The trial will be long and difficult, taking a great deal of time for the lawyers, judge, and other court officers.

Before the trial begins, there is a need for investigators to help both sides. Investigations may cost as much as $40,000.[2] There will be pretrial maneuvering, with both sides making motions, all of which takes more time.

Jury selection will take longer and involve more prospective jurors than other cases. Many potential jury members will not have the time or willingness to sit through a capital case. In addition, both defense and prosecution attorneys will be more likely to disqualify jurors because of the seriousness of the potential penalty. A California study found that jury selection took five times longer in capital cases. In Kansas, a district attorney estimated that impaneling a jury would take two weeks, compared to three days in noncapital cases.[3]

The trial is likely to use many different witnesses, including expensive experts, ranging from psychologists and pathologists to polygraph, fingerprint, and ballistics analysts. Each professional may charge hundreds of dollars or even thousands of dollars a day.[4]

If a conviction is obtained, there will be a presentencing report. This will require the time of expensive medical or psychological experts, again at costs of hundreds of dollars a day. There will be a separate hearing on the issue of the sentence. This translates into additional attorney's fees and other court costs. In a California study, it was estimated that capital trials were likely to last 3.5 times—about 30 days—longer than noncapital cases.[5] A study in Kansas showed that the typical trial phase of a capital case would cost $116,700 more than an ordinary murder trial.[6]

If a conviction is obtained and a death sentence given, the appeals process will begin. It will start in the state appellate courts, may move to the federal court system, then possibly back to the state again, then to the federal again, and so forth. During this process, many death sentences will be vacated either temporarily or permanently. If they are vacated temporarily, a new trial or a new sentence hearing may be required, adding to the costs. A New York study listed a minimum of ten stages of appeal and estimated that the process would typically take eight to ten years to complete.[7]

In the meantime, the defendant will be sitting in a cell on death row. He will be given a single cell and will be guarded one-on-one whenever he is moved from the cell. This requires a larger number of guards than is typical, even in maximum security. Any movement of the inmate to and from trial will also require additional personnel. The Kansas Department of Corrections estimated that it would cost almost $460,000 to create thirteen death row cells in their current facilities. They would also have to hire an additional twenty-three correctional officers, which in 1987 would have cost close to half a million dollars annually.

Finally, there is the cost of the execution itself. The prison will be put on special alert. The execution team will have to practice, which means that additional personnel will be brought in to cover the team members' usual duties. People who have special skills to prepare the execution apparatus may have to be hired. Extra personnel will be needed to control demonstrators, who will either protest or celebrate the execution. The prison may also need to have extra personnel to deal with heightened tension within the prison immediately before and after the execution. Special telephone lines running to the governor's office and the United States Supreme Court will need to be installed. Relevant courts will have to be kept on alert. With short stays, the process may take several weeks to complete. It was estimated that one aborted execution in Georgia cost more than $250,000.[8]

Both New York and Kansas conducted studies on the cost of capital punishment when they were considering re-establishing the death penalty in those states. In New York, it was estimated that reintroducing the death penalty would cost $118 million annually.[9] The Kansas study indicated that capital punishment would cost $11.4 million during the first year it was reintroduced, and that costs would increase each year as more and more inmates were placed on death row.[10]

Costs and Appeals

The high cost of capital punishment is created by the appeals process. The Furman decision created rigorous standards for applying the death penalty, because the Supreme Court recognized that death sentences were being giving in an arbitrary and capricious manner, often based on race. The appeals process helps to make sure capital sentences are applied with some minimum level of competence across the country.

This is important if there is to be a consistent standard of justice in our country. Certain judges are "hanging judges" while others are more lenient. The standards of racial justice in some places are much lower than in others. The appeals process helps these factors to be evened out across the country. The system is designed to assure that if two people are accused of similar crimes, they will be treated at least somewhat similarly. It does not assure fairness but does lead in that direction.

Appeals have overturned many death sentences that were given improperly. From January 1, 1973, through spring 1995, states placed 4,945 men and women on death row. Of that number, 1,530 have had their convictions or sentences overturned. This represents 31 percent of the total number originally sentenced to death. Of course, more convictions and sentences of the 3,009 people on death row in 1995 will be overturned. It is therefore safe to say that of all the people sentenced to death, about one-third will have their sentences changed through appeals. In the current political atmosphere, this is an amazing figure, because courts which may be reluctant to do so are still finding one-third of the death penalty sentences to be flawed and are overturning them.

But does the appeals process have to be so long and complicated? Of the thirty-one mistaken death sentences since the Furman decision cited by the book *In Spite of Innocence*, thirteen were not overturned in the first five years after the conviction. Eleven cases took eight years or more to be set right. Three took more than ten years to be corrected.[11] If the appeals process had been shortened, it is likely that some of these men would have been wrongly executed.

Conclusion

Studies have consistently shown that capital punishment is more expensive than keeping an offender in prison for life. The long period of appeals and the extra legal costs of death penalty cases add up. They mean that no money will be saved by executing an inmate rather than keeping him in prison. We give up the appeals process only at the risk of executing the innocent and making the death penalty process more arbitrary than it already is. In deciding to maintain the death penalty, our society has chosen to keep an ineffective crime-fighting method at huge cost. At the same time, we struggle to find money for education, housing, social services, and even other crime prevention measures—all likely to have a more positive effect on the crime rate than capital punishment.

14
The Effects on Society

Some capital punishment abolitionists argue that rather than deterring crime, executions create brutalizing effects on society that actually encourage people to be violent. As with the deterrence theory, there is no conclusive empirical proof for this argument. Some studies have tended to show that the number of murders does increase after an execution, but these statistics have by no means been conclusive.

My Experience During the Spenkelink Execution

In the short run, however, there can be little doubt that capital punishment has a brutalizing effect on the society that practices it. I was in Tallahassee, Florida, in May 1979 during the final days before the execution of John Spenkelink. Spenkelink was the first man executed against his own will after a decade in which no executions were carried out. (Gary Gilmore had voluntarily allowed the state of Utah to execute him two years earlier.)

During the month before Spenkelink's execution, I spent many hours in front of the governor's mansion, along with numerous other protesters against the death penalty. At first the demonstrations were quiet and peaceful. As the days wore on and it became apparent that the execution was going to be carried out, tension mounted. Counterdemonstrators began to show up. Discussions between the two groups quickly became arguments and then shouting matches. The first physical confrontation occurred when people began tearing down opposing signs that hung on the fence around the governor's mansion.

Each night the crowd was getting angrier. Finally one night, as I sat against the fence surrounding the governor's mansion, a fight broke out in front of me when a demonstrator tore a sign away from the hands of a counterdemonstrator.

The counterdemonstrators often showed up after the bars closed. They shouted derogatory chants about John Spenkelink and also about Ted Bundy, who had recently been arrested for the brutal rape-murder of two Florida State University coeds in Tallahassee and a young girl in Lake City, Florida. Most of the chants focused on the physical effects of the electric chair on the human body. One night a drunken counterdemonstrator began swinging a pool cue at the anti-death penalty protesters. A riot was averted only when cooler heads prevailed.

In the meantime, the anti-death penalty protesters were also becoming more violent. The focus of the protesters' anger was Governor Bob Graham. There was talk of stoning the governor's car when he entered and left the mansion.

Finally came the morning of May 25. It was clear that only a miracle would stop the execution. Early that morning a Jacksonville radio station dedicated a song to John Spenkelink. The song began with the sound of sizzling bacon. The chief protesters led a march to the governor's office. Once inside the capitol building, we waited for the news. Over a hundred people crowded into a couple of small entry rooms. Some protesters were standing on the furniture. As I looked around the room, I saw many people I had not seen before. These people had been attracted by the increasing excitement this morning.

When the news of John Spenkelink's electrocution finally came, many in the crowd started yelling. They wanted to trash the rooms we were in, break up the furniture, even set a fire. Again, only the cooler heads of the leadership averted a riot. They quickly moved a good part of the crowd out of the office. Without the support of the main body of protesters, the violent minority gave up and left as well.

As I think back on that time, I am amazed at the anger I felt, and the anger I saw in other people who believed in peace. The execution brought out the worst in most of us, as it did in those counterdemonstrators who favored capital punishment.

Celebrations of Death

From the days of public hangings to the present more sanitary approach of lethal injection behind closed doors, something about the execution process has excited emotions and fed anger. Capital punishment leads us to act without thinking. A man drives by anti-execution demonstrators and yells, "Fry the nigger." He wants to kill someone he does not know. Perhaps he knows nothing about the case except for the race of the man to be executed. Yet the act of the state killing this human being justifies his own anger, hatred, and racism. Something he might otherwise be ashamed of saying is shouted in public from a passing car for all to hear.

When the execution of James Autry was stopped at the last minute, the crowd of death penalty supporters shouted obscenities at the pro-death penalty attorney general who announced the stay. They chanted for the execution whenever the television cameras were turned on them.[1]

When Harold "Wili" Otey was electrocuted in Nebraska, drunken pro-death penalty crowds shouted racist slurs along with "U.S.A! U.S.A!" and "Go Big Red!"[2] The taking of human life was little more than a game. Thus the immediate effect of an execution on some people is not to turn them away from violence, but to turn them toward celebrating it.

Killing Becomes Easier

One of the tragedies of capital punishment is that the more executions carried out, the easier it becomes. When Gary Gilmore was executed in 1977 and John Spenkelink in 1979, it became national news. People protested the executions across the nation. Now newspapers give little notice to out-of-state executions. Only when an execution has some special attraction, such as protests against it made by important leaders or actors, does it merit more than local interest.

Death for Youthful Offenders. It also becomes easier to execute people who in the past may have been spared. Historically, there has been a movement away from executing juveniles. We still think with horror of how children were hung in eighteenth-century England. In recent years, however, there has been a trend away from protecting juvenile offenders. From 1973 to 1991, we saw 105 death sentences imposed on defendants aged seventeen years old or younger. This represents 2.4 percent of the total number of death sentences given during that period. Four of these sentences were carried out.[3]

Two important cases that affected youthful death sentencing procedures occurred in the late 1980s. In Thompson versus Oklahoma, on a five to four vote, the United States Supreme Court held that it was unconstitutional to execute children for crimes committed when they were less than sixteen years old. A year later in Stanford versus Kentucky, however, that Court held that the Eighth Amendment did not prohibit the imposition of the death penalty on people as young as sixteen years old. Death penalty opponents cannot be heartened by the fragile coalition that decided that no child under sixteen could be executed. With the current fear of youth gang violence, and the high level of support for the death penalty, there is reason to believe that a future court may allow the execution of children younger than sixteen.

However, polls have shown that Americans still give less support for executing youthful offenders than for executing adults. The following poll taken during the 1980s and 1990s shows that the public continues to have reservations about the imposition of the death penalty on minors.

State	Year	Support for the Death Penalty	
		In General	For Juveniles
California[4]	1989	79.5%	50%
Florida[5]	1986	84%	35%
Georgia#	1986	75%	53%
Kentucky[6]	1989	69.1%	42%
Oklahoma#	1988	80.2%	50%
National[7]	1994	80%	61%
National[8]	1995	78%	47%

#Cited in California poll results.

The Death Penalty and Politics

In 1988 George Bush made effective use of the fear of crime when he cited the case of Willie Horton against Michael Dukakis in the presidential campaign. Horton was an inmate who had been given a furlough from the Massachusetts prison system. While released, he raped and murdered a woman. Bush implied that the incident showed Dukakis was soft on crime. Bush's supporters also pointed to the fact that Massachusetts was a not a capital punishment state. They implied that since Dukakis did not favor the death penalty, he supported the rights of criminals over the public's safety.

In the current political climate, politicians who oppose capital punishment make easy targets for opponents. Bill Clinton recognized this and during the 1992 campaign hurried home to Arkansas to oversee the execution of Rickey Ray Rector. This man was so brain damaged by a self-imposed gunshot wound that he had the mental abilities of a six-year old child.[9]

The sadness of the Rickey Ray Rector story goes beyond the fact that then-Governor Clinton did not have the political courage to show mercy to a man who could clearly not understand what was happening to him. (After Rector was executed, prison officials found he had saved his dessert. He was planning to eat it later.) It is also symbolic, however, of how the issue of the death penalty has so supercharged the national debate on crime that more effective and humane solutions to the crime problem are ignored.

The typical anticrime package proposed by politicians who must show they are tough on criminals includes more and more expensive prisons, more retribution through mandatory sentencing, and fewer opportunities to appeal unjust convictions. The death penalty is the centerpiece. What the packages do not offer are preventive measures or alternatives to the punitive treatment of criminals. Such measures could effectively keep crimes from occurring or reduce recidivism by giving many prison inmates the economic and personal skills they need to pursue law-abiding lives. Yet these possibilities are ignored because the politicians do not wish to buck the public desire for revenge rather than rehabilitation.

Our failure to more seriously debate the crime issue is a fearful thing. We are opening the door for an erosion of rights through willingness to accept authoritarian measures to control crime. In reducing rights of criminals, we also reduce our own rights. Thus the long-term political effect of capital punishment and other retributive measures against crime may be to diminish freedom not just for criminals but for us all.

The Dictator's Tool

A great danger of capital punishment is that it can be and is used for political purposes. Internationally, the death penalty is used by many governments to legally dispose of people the government finds politically inconvenient.

Annually, Amnesty International issues a worldwide report on human rights abuses. This report includes instances where the death penalty was used for political purposes. In 1990, Amnesty reported that political prisoners were being held under death sentences in the following countries: Afghanistan, Albania, Algeria, Angola, Chile, China, Ethiopia, Indonesia, Iran, Iraq, Jordan, Liberia, Morocco, Nigeria, Pakistan, Somalia, Sudan, Trinidad and Tobago, Tunisia, Uganda, and Zimbabwe. In addition, numerous other governments used extrajudicial executions as a part of their unstated political policy.[10]

When we study this list of countries that continue to use the death penalty as opposed to those which no longer use it, we cannot help but conclude that the death penalty and oppression go hand in hand. Of the developed democracies, only the United States and Japan continue to use the death penalty. The death penalty is primarily used in countries which do not value free expression. Thus, until the fall of communism, the death penalty was an important political tool in eastern Europe. It is still used in many developing countries, as the list of countries who use it officially for political purposes shows.

Conclusion

The use of the death penalty has a brutalizing effect on society. It diminishes the importance of human life. It justifies hatred and bigotry. It often brings out the worst in both those who favor it and in those who oppose it. It has infected our political system by allowing our leaders to make symbolic gestures about crime prevention while they ignore the real causes of crime. Its continued use erodes human rights and thereby threatens us all.

15
Cruel and Unusual Punishment

Strict Constructionists and the Death Penalty

The current United States Supreme Court contains a number of conservative justices who like to call themselves "strict constructionists." They want to interpret the United States Constitution exactly as those who wrote it would have. They argue that if conditions have changed enough to warrant a different kind of interpretation, then the Constitution should be amended to reflect that change. Thus, for example, when American society as a whole no longer considered African-Americans subhumans fit only for slavery, the Constitution was amended to reflect this change in social attitude.

The strict constructionists on the Court therefore try to approach the issue of capital punishment as the Founding Fathers would have. Since the passage of the Eighth Amendment, which banned "cruel and unusual punishments," was not used to outlaw the death penalty in eighteenth-century America, these strict constructionists claim it cannot be used to outlaw capital punishment now.

This argument assumes that there was uniformity of opinion about what was cruel and unusual punishment in the eighteenth century, but history does not support this. While the majority believed in a harsh system of criminal justice, others did not. Beccaria attacked capital punishment in his influential *Essay on Crimes and Punishments* two decades before the Constitution was written. Benjamin Franklin, a member of the Constitutional Convention, had serious doubts about capital punishment, as did other early American leaders.

Let us, however, grant that most eighteenth-century Americans did approve of capital punishment. They also did not think the Eighth Amendment prohibited many other kinds of punishments that we consider cruel and unusual now. For example, flogging was practiced in eighteenth-century America, as was branding. Neither practice is now thought acceptable. The Constitution has not changed, but these punishments are considered cruel and unusual in twentieth-century America.

Moreover, the way capital punishment itself was practiced during the federalist period was different from what we consider acceptable now. There was mandatory capital sentencing for some crimes. This is no longer legal. There were many more capital crimes. Now we allow the death penalty only for murder and treason. Then very young children could be executed. We now say a child must be at least sixteen before he or she can be put to death. All these changes have occurred without a change in the Constitution.

The strict constructionists assume that the people who wrote the Constitution would not have changed with the times. This certainly was not the case. Many of our early leaders were extremely dynamic people who adapted readily to new conditions. They were revolutionaries and pragmatists. The Constitution for them was not an icon but a working document—to be interpreted according to the needs of the nation.

Unusual in the Western World

Therefore, we should not be asking whether eighteenth-century Americans would consider capital punishment to be cruel and unusual, but whether it should be considered to be cruel and unusual in the twentieth century.

In the two hundred years since the writing of the Constitution, we have learned much about human behavior. Modern psychology and sociology have given us new insights into why certain individuals become criminals. They have also given us new possibilities in the treatment of violent and antisocial behavior. What was once considered just "evil nature," we now recognize as a complex combination of physical, social, and psychological factors. Based on these new understandings, all Western democracies except the United States have stopped capital punishment. So in the Western world, at least, capital punishment is unusual.

Psychological Torture

However, is capital punishment cruel? There can be little doubt that it is. Dostoyevsky's description of the horror of waiting to be executed in *The Idiot* rings true for virtually everyone who reads it. In the American system, this horror is compounded by years of waiting. The waiting is done in solitary confinement. Death row inmates are kept in single cells and in some states are typically in their cells twenty-three hours each day. They have nothing to do except watch TV, read, or do handicrafts. They are given no productive work and have no one to talk to. They have virtually no physical contact with other human beings.

During this waiting, there will also be times when a "premature" execution date nears. Although everyone may be aware that the execution will be stayed, the prison officials are required to carry out procedures as if the execution will occur. The inmate is placed on "death watch." He may have to be shackled whenever he is moved from his cell. As the execution date approaches, he may be moved to an isolated death cell. Everyone knows the execution will not occur, but they all continue through the procedure until the stay is granted. The inmate is told to prepare for death and get family affairs in order. If the stay has not arrived forty-eight hours before execution, the inmate will be asked to choose a last meal. Officials will send for his spiritual adviser, if he has one, and they will summon his family.

If the stay comes very late, the inmate may have been completely prepared for death. This was the case in 1983, when the execution of Texas inmate James David Autry was stayed only twenty-four minutes before the planned lethal injection. Autry was already strapped onto the gurney on which he was expected to die. The intravenous tubes for injection were in his arm. He had said goodbye to his mother and brother, assuming he would never see them again.[1]

Such an experience brutally reminds the inmate of what may be in store for him. Even the most hardened observer must see this as a form of psychological torture.

When the actual execution finally occurs, it will be done in a ritualistic manner. During the prisoner's last few days, he will be under constant observation. Meticulous notes of his behavior will be kept. There will be a series of "last" steps, as described above.

Depending on the form of execution, he may have to be bodily prepared for the execution. For example, his head and parts of his body will be shaved if he is to be electrocuted. When the time finally comes, he will be visited by a chaplain or spiritual adviser, then taken to the execution room. He will be asked for his last words.

All this ritual surrounding the execution makes it more horrifying. The prisoner is constantly reminded of what will soon happen. He is forced to think about the coming execution with each last event. In criminal justice, combining this kind of ritualism with a killing is considered an aggravated form of murder. Yet this is the very kind of death the state imposes on those it executes.

Execution Methods and Botched Executions

Finally, there are the forms of execution themselves. The victim of the electric chair is literally burned to death from the inside out. As the electricity passes through his body, the places smolder where the electrodes are applied. In the case of Jessie Joseph Tafero, electrocuted in Florida's electric chair on May 4, 1990, fire, smoke, and sparks flew from his head.

Lawyers arguing against the use of the electric chair for a later execution claimed, "An inmate about to be executed in Florida will likely be burned and tortured during the execution, will be conscious during the event, and will suffer pain." Florida officials, after testing with a household toaster the flammability of the sponge used during the execution, declared that the appeal was "designed to distort Eighth Amendment issues with a smoke screen of technical and procedural faultfinding."[2]

Before Tafero's execution, a key prosecution witness recanted his testimony, then recanted his recantation—adding to Tafero's mental distress. After the execution, this witness recanted his testimony again, and another prosecution witness recanted her testimony. It was also found that the prosecution had withheld key evidence from the defense. All of this led the court to release Tafero's girlfriend and codefendant Sonia Jacobs from a life sentence and has cast doubt on Tafero's guilt.[3]

In another case, the execution took two jolts of electricity, with a total elapsed time of nineteen minutes for the execution. The first jolt of electricity in the execution of Horace Franklin Dunkins, a mentally retarded murderer condemned to death in Alabama, was given at 12:08 a.m. on July 14, 1989. When it was found that he had not been killed, a second jolt was applied at 12:17. Dunkins was not declared dead until ten minutes later. Alabama Prison Commissioner Morris Thigpen stated, "I regret very much what happened. It was human error. I just hope that he was not conscious and did not suffer."[4]

In the gas chamber, the victim is suffocated and poisoned. When the cyanide tablets begin to give off their fumes, he tries to hold his breath. When he can no longer do so, he gulps in the poison. As the cyanide takes effect, his body goes into convulsions, which may last several minutes. During this time, he may remain conscious.

Jimmy Lee Gray was executed in Mississippi on September 2, 1983. His attorney described the execution. "Jimmy Lee Gray died banging his head against a steel pole in the gas chamber while reporters counted his moans." Eight minutes after the gas was released, prison officials cleared the witnesses, so they would not see Gray's desperate attempts to breathe.

Describing the gas chamber execution of Donald Eugene Harding in Arizona, a television reporter stated, "I watched Harding go into violent spasms for fifty-seven seconds. Then he began to convulse frequently. His back muscles rippled. The spasms grew less violent. I timed them as ending six minutes and thirty-seven seconds after they began. His head went down in a little jerky motion. Obviously, the gentleman was suffering. This was a violent death, make no mistake about it."

Another account of Harding's death stated,

> When the fumes enveloped Don's head, he took a quick breath. A few seconds later he again looked in my direction. His face was red and contorted as if he were attempting to fight through tremendous pain. His mouth was pursed shut and his jaw was clenched tight. Don then took several more quick gulps of the fumes. At this point his body started convulsing violently. . . . His face and body fumed a deep red, and the veins in his temple and neck began to bulge until I thought they might explode. After about a minute Don's face leaned partially forward, but he was still conscious. Every few seconds he continued to gulp in. He was shuddering uncontrollably and his body was racked with spasms. . . . At this time the muscles along Don's left arm and back began twitching in a wavelike motion under his skin. Spittle drooled from his mouth. Don did not stop moving for approximately eight minutes, and after that he continued to twitch and jerk for another minute. Don Harding took ten minutes and thirty-one seconds to die.[5]

Finally, there is lethal injection. The victim is wheeled in on a hospital gurney. The executioner searches for a usable arm vein. This may be difficult because the veins may have been ruined by the use of intravenous drugs—both illegal and prescribed. It may take many minutes for a vein to be found.

When Rickey Ray Rector was executed in Arkansas on January 24, 1992, he offered to help the executioner because of the trouble the executioner was having to find a vein. It took the execution team fifty minutes to accomplish that task. Witnesses, who were held in an adjoining room and not allowed to view the procedure, reported hearing Rector groan numerous times throughout the process.

Stephen Peter Morin, executed in Texas on March 13, 1985, was probed in both arms and legs for 45 minutes. It took the execution team 47 minutes to find a vein on Billy Wayne White, another Texas inmate, executed on April 23, 1992.

Once the needle is inserted, other problems may occur. In the cases of Charles Walker (executed in Illinois, September 12, 1990), Emmitt Foster (executed in Missouri, May 4, 1994), and John Wayne Gacy (executed in Illinois, May 10, 1994), the lines carrying the execution chemicals clogged. In Walker's case, there was a kink in the line. In the other two cases, the arms with needles were bound so tightly that the chemicals could not flow. When Raymond Landry was executed in Texas on December 13, 1988, the needle pulled out of his arm two minutes after the chemicals began flowing. It took the execution team fourteen minutes to reinsert the needle.

There have been reports of violent reactions to the chemicals used for killing. When Stephen McCoy was executed in Texas on May 24, 1989, his chest heaved. He gasped and choked so violently that a witness fainted. A prison official was quoted, "The drugs may have been administered in a heavier dose or more rapidly."

The death of Robyn Lee Parks (executed in Oklahoma, March 10, 1992) looked "scary and ugly," according to a reporter. Parks' jaw, neck, and abdominal muscles spasmed for nearly a minute, while he gasped and gagged. Justin Lee May (executed in Texas, May 7, 1992) coughed and reared against the heavy restraints that held him down. According to one reporter, "He went into a coughing spasm, groaned and gasped, lifted his head from the death chamber gurney, and would have arched his back if he had not been belted down."[6]

The Other Victims

No matter what one may think of executing criminals, one group of innocent people is also punished. This is the inmate's family. It is hard for people who have never visited death row to realize that these men do have families. On my first visit to a death row inmate, the mother of one particularly notorious murderer was also visiting. I was shocked, because I had never thought of this man as someone's son or brother. A few weeks later I saw for the first time a child visit a death row inmate. The boy was the inmate's son. Both of these inmates have families, as do many other men and women on death row.

These family members are also victims of the death penalty, though innocent of any crime. Each time an execution date for their relative is set, they go through the agony of wondering if he will actually be killed. They follow the story in newspapers and on television. Parents wonder if there was anything they could have done differently and blame themselves.

They stand by helplessly as they see their child go through the torture of waiting for execution. They experience anger, fear, and depression. As the execution date nears, they are forced to make decisions about the disposal of the body. On the day of the execution, they visit. These last moments are awkward and painful. They hope the execution will somehow be stopped, even to the last moment. And then they grieve.

The execution makes the family famous for a brief time. If they have hidden the facts about their relative, insensitive strangers may ask them about it. Acquaintances may reject them. Children of an executed person may be teased viciously by other children. So the death penalty hurts not only the person executed but also family and friends.

Conclusion

No matter how humane we try to make the execution process, the death penalty always inflicts psychological torture on the person to be executed. Waiting to be killed cannot be made humane. The ritualistic nature of the execution process adds to this torture.

Nor can we ever be certain that the execution itself will not be botched. Human beings make mistakes, especially when they are in pressure situations, as killing another human being must always be. When mistakes are made, the person being executed suffers.

Capital punishment is also cruel to families of the offender. No one can watch a loved one being put to death without suffering. No matter how it is sugarcoated, an execution is a cruel and unusual event.

16
What Do We Want?

There is no proof, as this book shows, that capital punishment makes society safer. In fact, there is some evidence that capital punishment promotes violence. What then does the death penalty provide for us? It gives a false sense of doing something about crime. It gives us a brief sense of revenge for senseless acts of violence. And it titillates and excites us.

What price do we pay? Although capital punishment may meet some victim families' need for revenge, it is likely to prolong their suffering through its long and arduous process. Capital punishment exacerbates racism in our country and is used in discriminatory fashion against defendants who are mentally retarded. The poor are much more likely to receive a death sentence than the affluent, even when they commit similar crimes.

Mistakes are made. Innocent men and women are sometimes executed. The financial costs of capital punishment are extremely high. Executions do not lead us to value life but to devalue it. The death penalty is often a tool of tyranny. Demands for retribution against criminals may deprive us all of basic human rights. And no matter how humane we try to make an execution, it will always be a cruel act of violence.

All the countries of the Western world, except for the United States, have weighed the benefits of capital punishment against its costs and have done away with it. So we must ask ourselves, "What do we want?" Do we want to live in a society that encourages its members to devalue life and celebrates the killing of a fellow human being? Or do we want a society that is better than its worst members, and that believes that every person may be rehabilitated or redeemed?

Do we want a society willing to discriminate against its racial minorities, disabled, and poor even to the point of death? Or do we want a society that uses its resources to give all of its people the chance to live good, healthy, and productive lives?

Do we want to live in a society that takes innocent lives in order to revenge itself upon the guilty? Or do we want to live in a society that recognizes its own fallibility, and allows for its mistakes to be corrected?

Do we want a society that gives up basic human rights for a false sense of security? Or do we want to live in a society in which all citizens are protected by due process and the most basic human right—the right to life—is honored?

For Christian Readers

We have come full circle. This book began with religious arguments against the death penalty. Now we return to them. To answer "What do we want?" we must examine our beliefs about the purpose and value of human life. These beliefs must always rest on what we believe about the nature of the world.

For Christians, the ultimate reason for opposing the death penalty must rest on Jesus Christ, our executed Lord. His sacrifice on the cross gave all the human race the capability of being free from the sinfulness that infects our human nature. Through Jesus' death, we believe all humans have become redeemable.

In turning to Christ, we turn our backs on human idols that enthralled us in the past, idols we believed would protect us. We no longer depend on human systems for a false sense of security. We no longer accept our brutal impulses that would seek revenge and repudiate forgiveness.

Christ has offered us an opportunity to be fully human, in his image. But to grow up into spiritual maturity, we must offer the same opportunity to others. We cannot do that while still accepting what is most demeaning and vicious in our society.

If we are to fully accept the gift of life offered to us by our executed Lord, we can no longer support capital punishment, which is, in the final analysis, a glorification, worship, and idolization of death.

APPENDIXES

Important Legal Cases

Furman versus (v.) Georgia, 408 U.S. 238 (1972). The Supreme Court held that existing death penalty statutes did not provide sufficient guidance to judges and/or juries about when the death penalty should be applied. This decision vacated death sentences based on these laws, and required the states to write new death penalty legislation meeting much stricter standards. The decision is frequently referred to simply as "Furman" or "the Furman decision."

Gregg v. Georgia, 428 U.S. 153 (1976). The Supreme Court held that death penalty legislation following the guidelines outlined in Furman were constitutionally valid, thus reinstating the death penalty.

Ford v. Wainwright, 477 U.S. 399 (1986). The Supreme Court held that the death penalty cannot be inflicted on a person who is insane.

McCleskey v. Kemp, 481 U.S. 279 (1987). The United States Supreme Court accepted data that revealed prosecutors sought the death penalty in 70 percent of the cases where black defendants killed white people but in only 19 percent of the cases where white defendants were accused of murdering black victims. The majority opinion which upheld the death penalty described these disparities as "an inevitable part of our criminal justice system."

Thompson v. Oklahoma, 487 U.S. 815 (1988) prohibited the states from executing offenders for crimes committed when they were less than sixteen years old.

Stanford v. Kentucky, 492 U.S. 361 (1989) held that the Eighth Amendment does not prohibit the death penalty for crimes committed at sixteen or seventeen years old.

Penry v. Lynaugh, 109 St.Ct. 2934 (1989). The Supreme Court ruled that the death penalty for mentally retarded persons is not unconstitutional, but that mental retardation must be considered in selecting an appropriate penalty for a capital crime.

Herrera v. Collins, no. 91-7328, 52 Cr. L. Rpr. 3093 (1993). The Supreme Court held that a claim of innocence should not be considered in the federal appeals process unless the proof of innocence was not originally considered as the result of a procedural error.

Religious Statements Against the Death Penalty[1]

Baptist

American Baptist Churches in the U.S.A., Valley Forge, Pennsylvania 19482

Until the Gilmore case in 1977, there had been no execution in the United States in ten years. The ritual taking of life had ceased while debate continued in the courts regarding the constitutionality of capital punishment.

Now that the death penalty laws in some states have been upheld, over 400 persons nationwide face possible execution by hanging, firing squad, asphyxiation, or electrocution. Such punishment has been abolished in Canada and most of Europe, where it is seen as morally unacceptable and a form of cruel and unusual punishment inconsistent with religious and/or ethical traditions.

The majority of those on death row are poor, powerless, and educationally deprived. Almost 50 percent come from minority groups. This reflects the broad inequities within our society, and the inequity with which the ultimate punishment is applied. This alone is sufficient reason for opposing it as immoral and unjust.

Since further legal actions to stop executions appear unpromising, it is more important than ever that the religious community speak to the moral, religious, and ethical implications of killing by the state. Numerous secular and religious groups have recently taken positions in opposition to capital punishment.

THEREFORE, we as American Baptists, condemn the current reinstatement of capital punishment and oppose its use under any new or old state or federal law, and call for an immediate end to planned executions throughout this country.

We urge American Baptists in every state to act as advocates against the passage of new death penalty laws, and to act individually and in concert with others to prevent executions from being carried out.

We appeal to the governors of each state where an execution is pending to act with statesmanship and courage by commuting to life imprisonment without parole all capital cases within their jurisdiction.

—*Passed by the General Board of the American Baptist Churches, June 1977.*

Church of the Brethren
Church of the Brethren, 1451 Dundee Avenue, Elgin, Illinois 60120

We commend current efforts to abolish capital punishment and call upon Brethren everywhere to use their influence and their witness against it. —*Annual Conference, 1959.*

The Church of the Brethren General Board views with deep concern and alarm the resumption of the use of capital punishment. We affirm the Church of the Brethren Annual Conference Statements of 1957, 1959, and 1975 which uphold the sanctity of human life and personality, oppose the use of capital punishment, and encourage Brethren to work for the abolition of the death penalty.

We encourage Brethren to express their opposition to capital punishment, especially to governors and state legislators in states where capital punishment has been established or is being considered.

We deplore the taking of human life, whether by the hand of an individual or through the working of a judicial system. We pray, in the spirit of Jesus Christ who calls us to share his ministry of reconciliation, that our society will turn away from the use of capital punishment. —*General Board, 1979.*

The death penalty only continues the spiral of violence. Jesus said, "You have heard it said, 'An eye for an eye and a tooth for a tooth.' But I say to you, Do not resist one who is evil. But if anyone strikes you on the right cheek, turn to him the other also" (Matt. 5:38-39). Do we not believe this to be true? The only real way to deter further violence is to cease our claim to a "life for a life," to recognize that life and death decisions belong to God, and to seek mercy and redemption of God's lost children. . . .

In a broader sense, we Christians must lead the United States in a total commitment to nonviolence as public policy. All violent systems, structures, and ideologies should be challenged at their very core. . . .

Jesus came with a message of redemption and compassion for life, while the death penalty carries a message of condemnation and death.
—*Excerpts from a Statement of the 1987 Annual Conference of the Church of the Brethren.*

Disciples of Christ
Christian Church (Disciples of Christ), 130 East Washington Street, Indianapolis, Indiana 46204-3645

WHEREAS, there is currently a significant rise in the number of executions of convicted murderers throughout the United States, and

WHEREAS, public opinion polls suggest that a majority of the American public favor capital punishment for the purpose of deterring crime or for the purpose of retribution for violent acts, and

WHEREAS, the Holy Scriptures clearly mandate that we are not to kill, we are not to render evil for evil, and that we are not to seek retribution with vengeance for the evil done to us, and

WHEREAS, the use of execution to punish criminal acts does not allow for repentance or restitution of the criminal, and

WHEREAS, well-documented research clearly shows that capital punishment does not deter violent crime but may even give sanction to a climate of violence in our society, and

WHEREAS, the Christian Church (Disciples of Christ) meeting in conventions and General Assemblies has consistently approved resolutions that oppose capital punishment (1957-F11, 1962 #43, 1973 #44, and 1975 #34);

THEREFORE BE IT RESOLVED, that the congregations of the Christian Church be encouraged to utilize educational materials at every possible occasion to facilitate thoughtful discussion regarding the use of capital punishment, that each congregation in those states which have capital punishment statutes contact any elected legislator who is a member of the Christian Church (Disciples of Christ), making them aware of current statutes that permit the use of the death penalty, that those congregations communicate to their own Governor their encouragement and personal support of the Governor's use of his/her sentence to life imprisonment should an execution become imminent; and that all appropriate systems of influence be utilized to repeal all federal statutes which permit capital punishment.

—*Adopted by the 1985 General Assembly of the Disciples of Christ.*

Episcopal

The Protestant Episcopal Church U.S.A., 815 Second Avenue, New York, New York 10017

WHEREAS, the 1958 General Convention of the Episcopal Church opposed capital punishment on the theological basis that the life of an individual is of infinite worth in the sight of the Almighty God; and the taking of such a human life falls within the providence of Almighty God and not within the right of Man; and

WHEREAS, this opposition to capital punishment was reaffirmed at the General Convention of 1969; and

WHEREAS, a preponderance of religious bodies continue to oppose capital punishment as contrary to the concept of Christian love as revealed in the New Testament; and

WHEREAS, we are witnessing the reemergence of this practice as a social policy in many states; and

WHEREAS, the institutionalized taking of human life prevents the fulfillment of Christian commitment to seek redemption and reconciliation of the offender; and

WHEREAS, there are incarceration alternatives for those who are too dangerous to be set free in society; therefore be it

RESOLVED, the House of Bishops concurring this 66th General Convention of the Episcopal Church reaffirms its opposition to capital punishment and calls on all dioceses and members of this church to work actively to abolish the death penalty in their states; and be it further

RESOLVED, the House of Bishops concurring, that this 66th General Convention instruct the Secretary of General Convention to notify the several governors of the states of our action.

—*Statement of the 1979 General Convention; Reaffirmed in 1991. Reprinted courtesy of the Domestic and Foreign Missionary Society of the Protestant Episcopal Church U.S.A.*

Jewish
American Jewish Committee, East 65th Street, New York, NY 10022

WHEREAS capital punishment degrades and brutalizes the society which practices it; and

WHEREAS those who seek to retain the death penalty have failed to establish its deterrent effect or to recognize the fallibility of criminal justice institutions; and

WHEREAS capital punishment has too often been discriminatory in its application and is increasingly being rejected by civilized peoples throughout the world; and

WHEREAS we agree that the death penalty is cruel, unjust and incompatible with the dignity and self-respect of man;

NOW THEREFORE BE IT RESOLVED that the American Jewish Committee be recorded as favoring the abolition of the death penalty.

—*Adopted at the 66th Annual Meeting, May 6, 1972. Reproduced with the permission of the American Jewish Committee.*

Lutheran
Evangelical Lutheran Church, 8765 West Higgins Road, Chicago, Illinois 60631

A Social Practice Statement on the Death Penalty [A]
(See notes at end of this statement.)

A Climate of Violence

Violent crime is as ancient as the human family. Since Cain slew Abel, the blood of countless victims has cried out to the Lord. Our hearts, too, cry out to the Lord (Gen. 4:10) who gives life. We grieve with the family and friends of the victim—the violated one.

Violent crime has a powerful, corrosive effect on society. Bonds of trust, the very assumptions that allow us to live our lives in security and peace, break down. Instead of loving, we fear our neighbor. We especially fear the stranger.

The human community is saddened by violence, and angered by the injustice involved. We want to hold accountable those who violate life, who violate society. Our sadness and anger, however, make us vulnerable to feelings of revenge. Our frustration with the complex problems contributing to violence may make us long for simple solutions.

Such are the circumstances under which we, as the Evangelical Lutheran Church in America, speak to the death penalty. At the request of a number of congregations to synod assemblies, and in response to the memorials of those synods, the 1989 Churchwide Assembly placed the issue of the death penalty on the church's social agenda. Discussions on the death penalty then took place in local churches and at synodical and regional hearings.

Points of View

Members of the Evangelical Lutheran Church in America have different points of view with regard to social issues.[B] While the Spirit makes us one in our *faith in* the Gospel, we can and do vary in our *responses* to the Gospel.

While we all look to the Word of God and bring our reason to the death penalty issue, we can and do assess it with some diversity. Social statements of our church do not intend to end such diversity by "binding" members to a particular position.[C] Social statements acknowledge diversity and address members in their Christian freedom.

This church has not finished its deliberation on the death penalty. Members of the Evangelical Lutheran Church in America continue the deliberation, upholding together the authority of Scripture, creeds, and confessions; the value of God-given life; and the commitment to serve God's justice. Members continue their discussion, knowing they have in common the goals of justice, peace, and order.

As a church united in resistance to hate (Luke 6:11), we minister to an often vengeful society. As a Church united in joy over the good news of God's healing grace, we minister to a battered society. As a church heeding the call to do justice (Jer. 22:3), we minister to a broken society. As a church united for mission, we organize for ministries of restoration.

An Affirmation

On the basis of Scripture and the Lutheran Confessions, we hold that, through the divine activity of the Law, God preserves creation, orders society, and promotes justice in a broken world. God works through the state and other structures of society necessary for life in the present age.[D]

The state is responsible under God for the protection of its citizens and the maintenance of justice and public order. God entrusts the state with power to take human life when failure to do so constitutes a clear danger to society.

However, this does not mean that governments have an unlimited right to take life. Nor does it mean that governments must punish crime by death. We increasingly question whether the death penalty has been and can be administered justly.

Ministries of Restoration

Lutheran theological tradition has maintained that society is ruled by the Law and is influenced and nourished by the Gospel. Renewed by the Gospel, Christians, as salt of the earth (Matt. 5:13) [E] and light of the world (Matt. 5:14),[F] are called to respond to violent crime in the restorative way taught by Jesus (Matt. 5:38-39) [G] and shown by his actions (John 8:3-11).[H]

For the Evangelical Lutheran Church in America, following Jesus leads to a commitment to restorative justice. This commitment means addressing the hurt of each person whose life has been touched by violent crime. Restorative justice makes the community safer for all.

It Is Because of This Church's Ministry with and to People Affected by Violent Crime That We Oppose the Death Penalty. Executions focus on the convicted murderer, providing very little for the victim's family or anyone else whose life has been touched by the crime. Capital punishment focuses on retribution, sometimes reflecting a spirit of vengeance. Executions do not restore broken society and can actually work counter to restoration.

This church recognizes the need to protect society from people who endanger that society: removing offenders from the general population, placing them in a secure facility, and denying them the possibility of committing further crime (i.e., incapacitating them). Our challenge is to incapacitate offenders in a manner that limits violence, and holds open the possibility of conversion and restoration.

Doing Justice

Christians live in anticipation of the day when "justice roll [s] down like waters, and righteousness like an everflowing stream" (Amos 5:24). In the meantime, God holds governments accountable to ensure justice. In a democracy, where government is by the people, justice is the responsibility of all citizens.

Violent crime is, in part, a reminder of human failure to ensure justice for all members of society.[I] People often respond to violent crime as though it were exclusively a matter of the criminal's individual failure. The death penalty exacts and symbolizes the ultimate personal retribution.

Yet, capital punishment makes no provable impact on the breeding grounds of violent crime.[J] Executions harm society by mirroring and reinforcing existing injustice. The death penalty distracts us from our work toward a just society. It deforms our response to violence at the individual, familial, institutional, and systemic levels. It perpetuates cycles of violence.

It Is Because of This Church's Commitment to Justice That We Oppose the Death Penalty. Lutheran Christians have called for an assault on the root causes of violent crime,[K] an assault for which executions are no substitute. The ongoing controversy surrounding the death penalty shows the weaknesses of its justifications. We would be a better society by joining the many nations that have already abolished capital punishment.

Executions in the United States

Despite attempts to provide legal safeguards, the death penalty has not been and cannot be made fair. The race of the victim plays a role in who is sentenced to death and who is sentenced to life imprisonment,[L] as do the gender, race, mental capacity, age, and affluence of the accused. The system cannot be made perfect, for biases, prejudices, and chance affect whom we charge with a capital crime, what verdict we reach, and whether appeals will be successful.

Since human beings are fallible, the innocent have been executed in the past and will inevitably be executed in the future. Death is a different punishment from any other; the execution of an innocent person is a mistake we cannot correct.

It Is Because of This Church's Concern Regarding the Actual Use of the Death Penalty That We Oppose Its Imposition. The practice of the death penalty undermines any possible moral message we might want to "send." It is not fair and fails to make society better or safer. The message conveyed by an execution, reflected in the attention it receives from the public, is one of brutality and violence.[M]

Commitments of This Church

As a community gathered in faith, as a community dispersed in daily life, as a community of moral deliberation, and as a church body organized for mission, this church directs its attention to violent crime and the people whose lives have been touched by it.

As a community gathered in faith:

we welcome victims of violent crime and their families, standing with them and for them during their times of grief and anger;

we welcome offenders and their families, supporting them in their recovery;

we welcome partnership with faith communities within the correctional system, joining them in ministries of restoration;

we welcome people who work in criminal justice and their families, recognizing the special burden that accompanies such work.

As a community dispersed in daily life:

we continue to offer ministries of healing and reconciliation to victims of violent crime, to families of victims, and to neighborhoods that have experienced violence;

we recognize and affirm ministries by those who, in word and action, announce the good news to the imprisoned and their families;

we encourage the ministries conducted by people through their work in the criminal justice system;

we seek further opportunity to serve people caught in cycles of violence, and call for training to respond to the fear and anger of individuals, families, and society.

As a community of moral deliberation:

we invite and encourage moral deliberation on the causes and effects of criminal behavior, the function of punishment, and the role of the criminal justice system—a deliberation grounded in Scripture and informed by reason and knowledge, including the social sciences;

we shall discuss criminal justice in connection with other issues of concern to this church, such as racism, poverty, abuse, and chemical dependency;

we ask that available resource materials be distributed, and that a resource specific to the present statement be developed, printed, and distributed.

As a church organized for mission:

we recognize that the government bears responsibility for protecting people, and give it our support in the exercise of this function;

we commend public officials, and others, who shape the vision of a just society and work toward it;

we know the church is called by God to be a creative critic of the social order, and to speak on behalf of justice, peace, and order;

we urge the abolition of the death penalty, and support alternative and appropriate punishment for capital crime, including the possibility of life sentence without parole;

we call for an ongoing reform of the criminal justice system, seeking means of incapacitation that protect citizens while limiting violence and holding open the possibilities for conversion and restoration, and for education for future responsible citizenship in society;

we direct state public policy offices and the Lutheran Office for Governmental Affairs to work against the death penalty and for alternative and appropriate punishment for capital crime, such as imprisonment for natural life;

we ask congregations, synods, agencies, and institutions of this church to support the work of state advocacy offices and the Lutheran Office for Governmental Affairs in effecting the abolition of the death penalty;

we seek ways to work with our ecumenical partners, with other faith groups, and with other organizations with similar goals.

Notes

A. Social practice statements "focus on policy guidelines for the ELCA's responsibility in society. They are especially important in defining and developing priorities and directives for this church's advocacy and corporate social responsibility practices. In their use as teaching documents, their authority is persuasive, not coercive": "Social Statements in the Evangelical Lutheran Church in America," adopted by the 1989 Churchwide Assembly. On-line: http://www.elca.org/dcs/death.html

B. The following are issues reviewed during churchwide deliberation on the death penalty. They are offered here as a summary of points of view presented in the course of developing this statement. Members of the Evangelical Lutheran Church in America should be aware of them and may find some of them helpful for further discussion.

In Favor of the Death Penalty

Those who support the use of the death penalty often do so on the basis of Scripture, especially "you shall give life for life" (Exod. 21:23) and "let every person be subject to the governing authorities . . . for the authority does not bear the sword in vain" (Rom. 13:1-7; cf. 1 Pet. 2:13-14).

Proponents of the death penalty remind us that the Lutheran tradition has stressed the scriptural distinction between Law and Gospel, maintaining the right of the state under the realm of Law to punish evildoers.

Those who would retain the death penalty testify to the value of the life God has given and the murderer has taken; they assert the value of the victim's life by demanding the offender's death.

Supporters of the death penalty feel it makes society safer by permanently incapacitating convicted murderers.

Proponents argue that states have written death penalty statutes limiting the risk of error and meeting standards set by the United States Supreme Court.

Advocates of the death penalty claim it to have a deterrent effect, causing would be murderers to hesitate before taking actions that could result in the loss of their own lives.

In Opposition to the Death Penalty

Those who oppose the death penalty often do so on the basis of Scripture, arguing that Jesus in his teaching abolished the death penalty in the Law (Matt. 5:38-39, assuming the Sermon on the Mount applies not only to Christians but to all peoples) and by example (John 8:3-11).

Opponents of the death penalty note from Scripture and the confessions that God ordained government for the sake of good order, and oppose a practice they believe to be violent, unjust, and, therefore, contrary to good order.

Those who would abolish the death penalty observe that executions violate the sanctity of the offender's life, which God has given and which God values despite the repulsiveness of what the offender has done.

Opponents claim the state need not implement the death penalty to incapacitate safely those who threaten society, as attested by the international movement away from the death penalty and toward alternative and effective means of incapacitation.

Those who would abolish the death penalty assert that it continues to fall disproportionately upon those least able to defend themselves, and to run the risk of an irreparable mistake.

Arguing against the death penalty, people point to the unlikelihood of proving that the death penalty has a deterrent effect, and note that executions contribute to a climate of vindictiveness and violence.

C. For more on social statements, see "Social Statements in the Evangelical Lutheran Church in America" (full reference in note A, above).

D. "The Church in Society: A Lutheran Perspective," adopted by the 1991 Churchwide Assembly.

E. "You are the salt of the earth; but if salt has lost its taste, how can its saltiness be restored? It is no longer good for anything, but is thrown out and trampled under foot."

F. "You are the light of the world. A city built on a hill cannot be hid."

G. "You have heard that it was said, 'An eye for an eye and a tooth for a tooth.' But I say to you, Do not resist an evildoer. But if anyone strikes you on the right cheek, turn the other also."

H. The scribes and the Pharisees brought a woman who had been caught in the act of adultery; and making her stand before all of them, they said to him, "Teacher, this woman was caught in the very act of committing adultery. Now in the Law Moses commanded us to stone such women. Now what do you say?" They said this to test him, so that they might have some charge to bring against him. Jesus bent down and wrote with his finger on the ground. When they kept on questioning him, he straightened up and said to them, "Let anyone among you who is without sin be the first to throw a stone at her." And once again he bent down and wrote on the ground. When they heard it, they went away, one by one, beginning with the elders; and Jesus was left alone with the woman standing before him. Jesus straightened up and said to her, "Woman, where are they? Has no one condemned you?" She said, "No one, sir." And Jesus said, "Neither do I condemn you. Go your way, and from now on do not sin again." (On restoration, see also Matt. 5: [21-22] 23-24; Rom. 12:19-21; 1 Thess. 5:15; 1 Pet. 2:23.)

I. "In Pursuit of Justice and Dignity: Society, the Offender, and Systems of Correction," adopted by the Lutheran Church in America (1972).

J. The body of research on deterrent effect indicates, at best, conflicting evidence. Many proponents of the death penalty have abandoned the deterrence theory altogether, and argue for the death penalty on the basis of incapacitation or just retribution. Many opponents claim the death penalty stimulates crime, a claim for which there is also conflicting evidence.

K. "Capital Punishment," adopted by the Lutheran Church in America (1966), urged "the continued development of a massive assault on those social conditions, which breed hostility toward society and disrespect for the law." "Capital Punishment," adopted by The American Lutheran Church (1972), called for "the correction of conditions which contribute to crime."

L. The United States Supreme Court, in McCleskey v. Kemp (1987), acknowledged the findings of the David Baldus study in Georgia, which showed that the murderer of a white victim was more likely to receive a death sentence than the murderer of an African-American. The implication—that a white life is considered more valuable than an African-American life in the criminal justice system—has been of concern to the United States Congress in the drafting of racial justice legislation.

M. William J. Bowers and Glen J. Pierce, "Deterrence or Brutalization: What Is the Effect of Executions?" in *Crime and Delinquency* 26 (1980): 453-484.

—This social practice statement was adopted by a more than two-thirds majority vote at the second biennial Churchwide Assembly of the Evangelical Lutheran Church in America, meeting in Orlando, Florida, August 28-September 4, 1991. Reprinted from "ELCA Social Statement on the Death Penalty." Copyright © 1991, Evangelical Lutheran Church in America, and used by permission of Augsburg Fortress.

Mennonite
General Conference Mennonite Church, 722 Main Street, Box 347, Newton, Kansas 67114-0347

In view of our Christian responsibility to give witness to the righteousness which God requires of all men, we are constrained to set forth our convictions concerning capital punishment.

Our Belief
Since Christ through his redemptive work has fulfilled the requirement of the death penalty, and has given the church a ministry of reconciliation, and in view of the injustice and ineffectiveness of capital punishment as a means for the achievement of the purpose of government, we express our conviction that its use should be discontinued. In view of the prophetic commission given to the church, therefore, we appeal to the Parliament of the Dominion of Canada and to the federal and state governments of the United States, to discontinue the use of the death penalty and to set rehabilitation as the ultimate goal in the treatment of the criminal, expressing a positive attitude to the offender, thus further encouraging the peace and order which under the lordship of Christ the state is commissioned to provide.

Our Confession and Our Prayer
In view of our responsibility as ministers of reconciliation, we confess that we have not adequately fulfilled our obligation to work for the abolition of capital punishment or for the reduction of crime in our society. We need to be more faithful in serving persons in prison and in laboring for the reform of prison procedures; for the rehabilitation of released prisoners; and for the improvement of economic, social, and religious conditions which contribute to the making of juvenile offenders and to the spread of crime.

We pray that in our brotherhood the Spirit may deepen each member's conviction and understanding of his obligation to individual criminal offenders, to the government under which he lives, and to Christ. And we pray that God may grant us wisdom, vision, and courage that as a brotherhood we may engage in this ministry as the Holy Spirit gives us direction.

—*Adopted by the General Conference Mennonite Church, meeting at Estes Park, Colorado, July 16, 1965.*

The Mennonite Church, 528 E. Madison Street, Lombard, Illinois 60148

In view of the prophetic commission given to the church as set forth in two recent statements of Mennonite General Conference, *A Declaration of Christian Faith and Commitment with Respect to War, Peace, and Non-Resistance* (1951), and *The Christian Witness to the State* (1961); in view of the sanctity of human life; and in view of our redemptive concern for the offender, be it

RESOLVED that we appeal to the Parliament of the Dominion of Canada and to the federal and state governments of the United States, to discontinue the use of the death penalty and that we refer to our conferences and congregations for study and discussion, the paper, "A Christian Declaration on Capital Punishment," as prepared by the Peace Problems Committee.

In view of our responsibility as ministers of reconciliation, be it further

RESOLVED that we confess that we have not adequately fulfilled our obligation to the offender nor for the reduction of crime in our society. We need to be more faithful in bringing the Christian witness to persons in prison and in laboring for the reform of prison procedures, for the rehabilitation of released prisoners, and for the correction of economic, social, and religious conditions which contribute to the making of juvenile offenders and to the spread of crime.

We pray that in our brotherhood the Spirit may deepen each member's conviction and understanding of his obligation to individual criminal offenders, to the government under which he lives, and to Christ. And we pray that God may grant us wisdom, vision, and courage that as a brotherhood we may engage in this ministry as the Holy Spirit gives us direction.

—*Adopted by the Mennonite Church, meeting at Kidron, Ohio, August 1965.*

Methodist

The United Methodist Church, Board of Church and Society, 100 Maryland Avenue, N.E., Washington, D.C. 20002

In spite of the common assumption to the contrary, "an eye for an eye and a tooth for a tooth," does not give justification for imposing the penalty of death. Jesus explicitly repudiated the *lex talionis* (Matt. 5:38-39), and the Talmud denies its literal meaning and holds that it refers to financial indemnities.

When a woman was brought before Jesus, having committed a crime for which the death penalty was commonly imposed, our Lord so persisted in questioning the moral authority of those who were ready to conduct the execution, that they finally dismissed the charges (John 8:9).

The Social Principles statement of the United Methodist Church condemns ". . . torture of persons by governments for any purpose," and asserts that it violates Christian teachings. The church through its Social Principles further declares, "We oppose capital punishment and urge its elimination from all criminal codes."

. . . .The United Methodist Church cannot accept retribution or social vengeance as a reason for taking human life. It violates our deepest belief in God as the Creator and the Redeemer of humankind. In this respect, there can be no assertion that human life can be taken humanely by the state. Indeed, in the long run, the use of the death penalty by the state will increase the acceptance of revenge in our society and will give official sanction to a climate of violence.

The United Methodist Church is deeply concerned about the present high rate of crime in the United States, and about the value of life taken in murder or homicide. When another life is taken through capital punishment, the life of the victim is further devalued. Moreover, the church is convinced that the use of the death penalty would result in neither a net reduction of crime in general nor in a lessening of the particular kinds of crime against which it is directed. Homicide—the crime for which the death penalty has been used almost exclusively in recent decades—increased far less than other major crimes during the period of the moratorium. Progressively rigorous scientific studies, conducted over more than forty years, overwhelmingly failed to support the thesis that capital punishment deters homicide more effectively than does imprisonment. . . .

The death penalty also falls unfairly and unequally upon an outcast minority. Recent methods for selecting the few persons sentenced to die from among the larger number who are convicted of comparable offenses have not cured the arbitrariness and discrimination that have historically marked the administration of capital punishment in this country.

The United Methodist Church is convinced that the nation's leaders should give attention to the improvement of the total criminal justice system and to the elimination of social conditions that breed crime and cause disorder, rather than fostering a false confidence in the effectiveness of the death penalty.

The United Methodist Church declares its opposition to the retention and use of capital punishment in any form or carried out by any means; the church urges the abolition of capital punishment.

—Adopted by the 1980 General Conference of the United Methodist Church. Excerpted and reprinted from "Capital Punishment," *from* The Book of Resolutions of the United Methodist Church 1980, *copyright © 1980 by the United Methodist Publishing House, and used by permission.*

Moravian

The Moravian Church, 1021 Center Street, P.O. Box 1245,
Bethlehem, Pennsylvania 18016-1245

Resolved, that the Northern Province of the Moravian Church in North America put itself on record as being opposed to capital punishment and that members of the Moravian church be urged to work for the abolition of the death penalty.

—*Adopted by the 1961 Synod of the Moravian Church.*

Presbyterian

Presbyterian Church (U.S.A.), 100 Witherspoon Street,
Louisville, Kentucky 40202

Whereas, the 171st General Assembly (United Presbyterian Church—1959) declared that "capital punishment cannot be condoned by an interpretation of the Bible based upon the revelation of God's love in Jesus Christ . . ." and "The use of the death penalty tends to brutalize the society that condones it"; the 177th General Assembly (UPC—1965) called for the abolition of the death penalty; the 106th General Assembly (Presbyterian Church U.S.—1966) proclaimed itself against the death penalty; and the 189th General Assembly (UPC—1977) called upon members to work to prevent executions of persons under sentence of death, to work against efforts to reinstate death penalty statutes, and to work for alternatives to capital punishment; and

Whereas, we believe the government's use of death as an instrument of justice places the state in the role of God, who alone is sovereign; and

Whereas, the use of the death penalty in a representative democracy places citizens in the role of executioner: "Christians cannot isolate themselves from corporate responsibility, including responsibility for every execution, as well as for every victim" (UPC—1977); and

Whereas, since between July 2, 1976, when the U.S. Supreme Court ruled in *Gregg v. Georgia* that capital punishment "does not invariably violate the Constitution," and as of September 30, 1984, 38 states have approved death penalty statutes and have executed 26 persons; and

Whereas, there are presently over 1,400 persons on death row in the U.S., many of whose rights of appeal are rapidly running out:

Therefore, the 197th General Assembly (1985):

1. Reaffirms the positions of the General Assemblies of the United Presbyterian Church of 1959, 1965, and 1977, and of the Presbyterian Church U.S. of 1966, and declares its continuing opposition to capital punishment.

2. Calls upon governing bodies and members to work for the abolition of the death penalty in those states which currently have capital punishment statutes, and against efforts to reinstate such statutes in those which do not.

3. Urges continuing study of issues related to capital punishment and

commends the use of resources available from the Presbyterian Criminal Justice Program.

4. Requests the stated clerk to notify the president and the Congress of the United States, and all the state governors and legislatures, of the action taken.

—*Adopted by the 1985 General Assembly of the Presbyterian Church (U.S.A.)*

Reformed

Reformed Church in America, 475 Riverside Drive, 18th Floor, New York, New York 10115

That in light of the following reasons this General Synod go on record as opposing the retention of capital punishment as an instrument of justice within our several states, encouraging forward-looking study in all areas related to criminology; supporting all efforts to improve our penal institutions, crime prevention agencies and policy procedures, and efforts being made to secure provision of adequate staff and budget for prisons, parole boards, and similar institutions:

1. Capital punishment is incompatible with the spirit of Christ and the ethic of love.

2. Capital punishment is of doubtful value as a deterrent.

3. Capital punishment results in inequities in application.

4. Capital punishment is a method subject to irremediable mistakes.

5. Capital punishment ignores corporate and community guilt.

6. Capital punishment perpetuates the concepts of vengeance and retaliation.

7. Capital punishment ignores the entire concept of rehabilitation. The Christian faith should be concerned not with retribution, but with redemption.

—*Adopted by the 1965 General Synod of the Reformed Church in America.*

Roman Catholic

U.S. Catholic Conference, Committee on Social Development and World Peace, 3211 Fourth Street N.E., Washington, D.C. 20017-1194

U.S. Catholic Bishops' Statement on Capital Punishment

Introduction

In 1974, out of a commitment to the value and dignity of human life, the U.S. Catholic Conference, by a substantial majority, voted to declare its opposition to capital punishment. As a former president of the National Conference of Catholic Bishops pointed out in 1977, the issue of capital punishment involves both "profound legal and political questions" as well as "important moral and religious issues" [A] (see notes at end of this statement). And so we find that this issue continues to provoke public controversy and to raise moral questions that trouble many. This is particularly true in the aftermath of widely publicized executions in Utah and Florida and as a result of public realization that there are now over five hundred persons awaiting execution in various prisons in our country.

The resumption of capital punishment after a long moratorium, which began in 1967, is the result of a series of decisions by the United States Supreme Court. In the first of these decisions, *Furman v. Georgia* (1972), the Court held that the death penalty as then administered did constitute cruel and unusual punishment and so was contrary to the Eighth Amendment to the Constitution. Subsequently in 1976 the Court upheld death sentences imposed under state statutes which had been revised by state legislatures in the hope of meeting the Court's requirement that the death penalty not be imposed arbitrarily. These cases and the ensuing revision of state and federal statutes gave rise to extended public debate over the necessity and advisability of retaining the death penalty. We should note that much of this debate was carried on in a time of intense public concern over crime and violence. For instance, in 1976 alone, over 18,000 people were murdered in the United States. Criticism of the inadequacies of the criminal justice system has been widespread, even while spectacular crimes have spread fear and alarm, particularly in urban areas. All these factors make it particularly necessary that Christians form their views on this difficult matter in a prayerful and reflective way and that they show a respect and concern for the rights of all.

We should acknowledge that in the public debate over capital punishment we are dealing with values of the highest importance: respect for the sanctity of human life, the protection of human life, the preservation of order in society, and the achievement of justice through law. In confronting the problem of serious and violent crime in our society, we want to protect the lives and the sense of security both of those members of society who may become the victims of crime and of those in the police and in the law enforcement system who run greater risks. In doing this, however, we must bear in mind that crime is both a manifestation of the great mysteries of evil and human freedom and an aspect of the very complex reality that is contemporary society. We should not expect simple or easy solutions to what is a profound evil, and even less should we rely on capital punishment to provide such a solution. Rather, we must look to the claims of justice as these are understood in the current debate and to the example and teaching of Jesus, whom we acknowledge as the Justice of God.

I. *Purposes of Punishment*

Allowing for the fact that Catholic teaching has accepted the principle that the state has the right to take the life of a person guilty of an extremely serious crime, and that the state may take appropriate measures to protect itself and its citizens from grave harm, nevertheless, the question for judgment and decision today is whether capital punishment is justifiable under present circumstances. Punishment, since it involves the deliberate infliction of evil on another, is always in need of justification. This has normally taken the form of indicating some good which is to be obtained through punishment or an evil which is to be warded off. The three justifications traditionally advanced for punishment in general are retribution, deterrence, and reform.

Reform or rehabilitation of the criminal cannot serve as a justification for capital punishment, which necessarily deprives the criminal of the opportunity to develop a new way of life that conforms to the norms of society and that contributes to the common good. It may be granted that the imminence of capital punishment may induce repentance in the criminal, but we should certainly not think that this threat is somehow necessary for God's grace to touch and to transform human hearts.

The deterrence of actual or potential criminals from future deeds of violence by the threat of death is also advanced as a justifying objective of punishment. While it is certain that capital punishment prevents the individual from committing further crimes, it is far from certain that it actually prevents others from doing so. Empirical studies in this area have not given conclusive evidence that would justify the imposition of the death penalty on a few individuals as a means of preventing others from committing crimes. There are strong reasons to doubt that many crimes of violence are undertaken in a spirit of rational calculation which would be influenced by a remote threat of death. The small number of death sentences in relation to the number of murders also makes it seem highly unlikely that the threat will be carried out and so undercuts the effectiveness of the deterrent.

The protection of society and its members from violence, to which the deterrent effect of punishment is supposed to contribute, is a value of central and abiding importance; and we urge the need for prudent firmness in ensuring the safety of innocent citizens. It is important to remember that the preservation of order in times of civil disturbance does not depend on the institution of capital punishment, the imposition of which rightly requires a lengthy and complex process in our legal system. Moreover, both in its nature as legal penalty and in its practical consequences, capital punishment is different from the taking of life in legitimate self-defense or in defense of society.

The third justifying purpose for punishment is retribution or the restoration of the order of justice which has been violated by the action of the criminal. We grant that the need for retribution does indeed justify punishment. For the practice of punishment both presupposes a previous transgression against the law and involves the involuntary deprivation of certain goods. But we maintain that this need does not require nor does it justify taking the life of the criminal, even in cases of murder. We must not remain unmindful of the example of Jesus, who urges upon us a teaching of forbearance in the face of evil (Matt. 5:38-42) and forgiveness of injuries (Matt. 18:21-35). It is morally unsatisfactory and socially destructive for criminals to go unpunished, but the forms and limits of punishment must be determined by moral objectives which go beyond the mere inflicting of injury on the guilty. Thus we would regard it as barbarous and inhumane for a criminal who had tortured or maimed a victim to be tortured or maimed in return. Such a punishment might satisfy certain vindictive desires that we or the victim might feel, but the satisfaction of such desires is not and cannot be an objective of a humane and Christian approach to punishment. We believe that the forms of punishment must be determined with a view to the protection of society and its members and to the reformation of the criminal and his reintegration into society (which may not be possible in certain cases). This position accords with the general norm for punishment proposed by St. Thomas Aquinas when he wrote: "In this life, however, penalties are not sought for their own sake, because this is not the era of retribution; rather, they are meant to be corrective by being conducive either to the reform of the sinner or the good of society, which becomes more peaceful through the punishment of sinners." [8]

We believe that in the conditions of contemporary American society, the legitimate purposes of punishment do not justify the imposition of the death penalty. Furthermore, we believe that there are serious considerations which should prompt Christians and all Americans to support the abolition of capital punishment. Some of these reasons have to do with evils that are present in the practice of capital punishment itself, while others involve important values that would be promoted by abolition of this practice.

II. Christian Values in the Abolition of Capital Punishment

We maintain that abolition of the death penalty would promote values that are important to us as citizens and as Christians. First, abolition sends a message that we can break the cycle of violence, that we need not take life for life, that we can envisage more humane and more hopeful and effective responses to the growth of violent crime. It is a manifestation of our freedom as moral persons striving for a just society. It is also a challenge to us as a people to find ways of dealing with criminals that manifest intelligence and compassion rather than power and vengeance. We should feel such confidence in our civic order that we use no more force against those who violate it than is actually required.

Second, abolition of capital punishment is also a manifestation of our belief in the unique worth and dignity of each person from the moment of conception, a creature made in the image and likeness of God. It is particularly important in the context of our times that this belief be affirmed with regard to those who have failed or whose lives have been distorted by suffering or hatred; even in the case of those who by their actions have failed to respect the dignity and rights of others. It is the recognition of the dignity of all human beings that has impelled the Church to minister to the needs of the outcast and the rejected and that should make us unwilling to treat the lives of even those who have taken human life as expendable or as a means to some further end.

Third, abolition of the death penalty is further testimony to our conviction, a conviction which we share with the Judaic and Islamic traditions, that God is indeed the Lord of life. It is a testimony which removes a certain ambiguity which might otherwise affect the witness that we wish to give to the sanctity of human life in all its stages. We do not wish to equate the situation of criminals convicted of capital offenses with the condition of the innocent unborn or of the defenseless aged or infirm, but we do believe that the defense of life is strengthened by eliminating exercise of a judicial authorization to take human life.

Fourth, we believe that abolition of the death penalty is most consonant with the example of Jesus, who both taught and practiced the forgiveness of injustice and who came "to give his life a ransom for many" (Mark 10:45). In this regard we may point to the reluctance which those early Christians who accepted capital punishment as a legitimate practice in civil society felt about the participation of Christians in such an institution [c] and to the unwillingness of the church to accept into the ranks of its ministers those who had been involved in the infliction of capital punishment.[D] There is and has been a certain sense that even in those cases where serious justifications can be offered for the necessity of taking life, those who are identified in a special way with Christ should refrain from taking life. We believe that this should be taken as an indication of the deeper desires of the church as it responds to the story of God's redemptive and forgiving love as manifest in the life of his Son.

III. Difficulties Inherent in Capital Punishment

With respect to the difficulties inherent in capital punishment, we note first that infliction of the death penalty extinguishes possibilities for reform and rehabilitation for the person executed as well as the opportunity for the criminal to make some creative compensation for the evil he or she has done. It also cuts off the possibility for a new beginning and of moral growth in a human life which has been seriously deformed.

Second, the imposition of capital punishment involves the possibility of mistake. In this respect, it is not different from other legal processes; and it must be granted our legal system shows considerable care for the rights of defendants in capital cases. But the possibility of mistake cannot be eliminated from the system. Because death terminates the possibilities of conversion and growth and support that we can share with each other, we regard a mistaken infliction of the death penalty with a special horror, even while we retain our trust in God's loving mercy.

Third, the legal imposition of capital punishment in our society involves long and unavoidable delays. This is in large part a consequence of the safeguards and the opportunities for appeal which the law provides for defendants; but it also creates a long period of anxiety and uncertainty both about the possibility of life and about the necessity of reorienting one's life. Delay also diminishes the effectiveness of capital punishment as a deterrent, for it makes the death penalty uncertain and remote. Death row can be the scene of conversion and spiritual growth, but it also produces aimlessness, fear, and despair.

Fourth, we believe that the actual carrying out of the death penalty brings with it great and avoidable anguish for the criminal, for his family and loved ones, and for those who are called on to perform or to witness the execution. Great writers such as Shakespeare and Dostoyevsky in the past and Camus and Orwell in our time have given us vivid pictures of the terrors of execution not merely for the victim but also for bystanders.[E]

Fifth, in the present situation of dispute over the justifiability of the death penalty and at a time when executions have been rare, executions attract enormous publicity, much of it unhealthy, and stir considerable acrimony in public discussion. On the other hand, if a substantial proportion of the more than five hundred persons now under sentence of death are executed, a great public outcry can safely be predicted. In neither case is the American public likely to develop a sense that the work of justice is being done with fairness and rationality.

Sixth, there is a widespread belief that many convicted criminals are sentenced to death in an unfair and discriminatory manner. This belief can be affirmed with certain qualifications. There is a certain presumption that if specific evidence of bias or discrimination in sentencing can be provided for particular cases, then higher courts will not uphold sentences of death in these cases. But we must also reckon with a legal system which, while it does provide counsel for indigent defendants, permits those who are well off to obtain the resources and the talent to present their case in as convincing a light as possible. The legal system and the criminal justice system both work in a society which bears in its psychological, social, and economic patterns the marks of racism. These marks remain long after the demolition of segregation as a legal institution. The end result of all this is a situation in which those condemned to die are nearly always poor and are disproportionately black.[F] Thus 47 percent of the inmates on death row are black, whereas only 11 percent of the American population is black. Abolition of the death penalty will not eliminate racism and its effects, an evil which we are called on to combat in many different ways. But it is a reasonable judgment that racist attitudes and the social consequences of racism have some influence in determining who is sentenced to die in our society. This we do not regard as acceptable.

IV. Conclusions

We do not propose the abolition of capital punishment as a simple solution to the problems of crime and violence. As we observed earlier, we do not believe that any simple and comprehensive solution is possible. We affirm that there is a special need to offer sympathy and support for the victims of violent crime and their families. Our society should not flinch from contemplating the suffering that violent crime brings to so many when it destroys lives, shatters families, and crushes the hopes of the innocent. Recognition of this suffering should not lead to demands for vengeance but to a firm resolution that help be given to the victims of crime and that justice be done fairly and swiftly. The care and the support that we give to the victims of crime should be both compassionate and practical. The public response to crime should include the relief of financial distress caused by crime and the provision of medical and psychological treatment to the extent that these are required and helpful. It is the special responsibility of the church to provide a community of faith and trust in which God's grace can heal the personal and spiritual wounds caused by crime and in which we can all grow by sharing one another's burdens and sorrows.

We insist that important changes are necessary in the correctional system in order to make it truly conducive to the reform and rehabilitation of convicted criminals and their reintegration into society.[G] We also grant that special precautions should be taken to ensure the safety of those who guard convicts who are too dangerous to return to society. We call on governments to cooperate in vigorous measures against terrorists who threaten the safety of the general public and who take the lives of the innocent. We acknowledge that there is a pressing need to deal with those social conditions of poverty and injustice which often provide the breeding grounds for serious crime. We urge particularly the importance of restricting the easy availability of guns and other weapons of violence. We oppose the glamorizing of violence in entertainment, and we deplore the effect of this on children. We affirm the need for education to promote respect for the human dignity of all people. All of these things should form part of a comprehensive community response to the very real and pressing problems presented by the prevalence of crime and violence in many parts of our society.

We recognize that many citizens may believe that capital punishment should be maintained as an integral part of our society's response to the evils of crime, nor is this position incompatible with Catholic tradition. We acknowledge the depth and the sincerity of their concern. We urge them to review the considerations we have offered which show both the evils associated with capital punishment and the harmony of the abolition of capital punishment with the values of the gospel. We urge them to bear in mind that public decisions in this area affect the lives, the hopes, and the fears of men and women who share both the misery and the grandeur of human life with us and who, like us, are among those sinners whom the Son of Man came to save.

We urge our brother and sisters in Christ to remember the teaching of Jesus, who called us to be reconciled with those who have injured us (Matt. 5:43-45) and to pray for forgiveness for our sins "as we forgive those who have sinned against us" (Matt. 6:12). We call on you to contemplate the crucified Christ, who set us the supreme example of forgiveness and of the triumph of compassionate love.

Notes

A. *Statement on Capital Punishment*, Archbishop Joseph L. Bernardin, President National Conference of Catholic Bishops, January 26, 1977. Cf. *Community and Crime*, Statement of the Committee on Social Development and World Peace, United States Catholic Conference, February 15, 1978, p. 8.

B. Thomas Aquinas, *Summa Theologiae*, II-II, 68, 1; trans. Marcus Lefebvre, O.P. (London: Blackfriars, 1975).

C. Tertulliam, *De Idolatria*, c. 17.

D. Code of Canon Law, Canon 984.

E. William Shakespeare, *Measure for Measure*, Act II, Scene 1; Fyodor Dostoyevsky, *The Idiot*; George Orwell, "A Hanging"; Albert Camus, "Reflections on the Guillotine."

F. Cf. Charles Black Jr., *Capital Punishment* (New York: Norton, 1974), pp. 84-91.

G. Cf. *The Reform of Correctional Institutions in the 1970s*, Statement of the United States Catholic Conference, November 1973.

—*Approved by the U.S. Bishops in November 1980. Copyright © 1980 U.S. Catholic Conference Inc., and used with permission, all rights reserved. On-line: http://www2.pbs.org/wgbh/pages/frontline/angel/procon/bishopstate.html*

Society of Friends (QUAKER)

Friends United Meeting, 101 Quaker Hill Drive, Richmond, Indiana 47374

Friends accept the biblical teachings that every human life is valuable in the sight of God, that man need not remain in his sinful state but can repent and be saved, that God loves the sinner and takes "no pleasure in the death of the wicked," but longs "that the wicked turn from their ways and live" (Ezek. 33:11).

We oppose capital punishment because it violates the gospel we proclaim, and promotes the evils of vengeance and injustice through the agencies of government intended to advance righteousness and justice. We believe the Christian way to deal with crime is to seek the redemption and rehabilitation of the offender, promote penal reform, and work diligently at the task of preventing crime.

As capital punishment is abolished, we recognize that society must be protected against release from prison of those unredeemed in spiritual life or whose condition of physical or mental health would endanger others.

We look with favor upon the renewed efforts in our time to abolish capital punishment, urge our members individually, and our Monthly and Yearly Meetings to unite with others in the task for removing the death penalty from the statute books of the various states, provinces, central or federal governments, and the United Nations.

—*Approved at Five Years Meeting of Friends, July 21, 1960.*

Friends Committee on National Legislation, 245 Second Street, N.E., Washington, D.C. 20002

We seek the abolition of the death penalty because it denies the sacredness of human life and violates our belief in the human capacity to change. This irreversible penalty cannot be applied equitably and without error. Use

of the death penalty by the state powerfully reinforces the idea that killing can be a proper way of responding to those who have wronged us. We do not believe that reinforcement of that idea can lead to healthier and safer communities.
—*Statement of Legislative Policy of the Society of Friends, November 12, 1994.*

Unitarian

Unitarian Universalist Association, 25 Beacon Street,
Boston, Massachusetts 02108

WHEREAS, General Assemblies to the Unitarian Universalist Association have opposed capital punishment by Resolution in 1961, 1966, and 1974; and

WHEREAS, the aforementioned Resolutions have urged complete abolition of capital punishment as inconsistent with respect for human life; for its retributive, discriminatory, and non-deterrent character; and opposed its restoration or continuance in any form; and

WHEREAS the State of Florida has declared its intent to proceed with executions of those under capital sentence in Florida prisons, numbering more than one hundred, and having begun with the execution of John Spenkelink on May 25, 1979; and

WHEREAS, the Florida example may become precedent for a new wave of capital punishment in numerous other states;

BE IT RESOLVED: That the 1979 General Assembly of the Unitarian Universalist Association urges the Governor of the State of Florida to commute all existing death sentences; and

BE IT FURTHER RESOLVED: That the General Assembly urges governors of all other states similarly to commute death sentences and to prevent the restoration or continuance of capital punishment.
—*Passed by the 1979 General Assembly of the Unitarian Universalist Association.*

United Church of Christ

The United Church of Christ, 700 Prospect Avenue, Cleveland, Ohio 44115

WHEREAS the Seventh, Ninth, and Eleventh General Synods of the United Church of Christ have declared their opposition to the death penalty as a means of restorative justice; and

WHEREAS such opposition is based on our understanding of the Christian faith and the New Testament call to redemptive love, mercy, and sanctity of life; and

WHEREAS the death penalty has now been reinstated in thirty-five states resulting in 520 people being confined to death row—132 of whom reside in the Florida State Prison; and

WHEREAS it has been demonstrated that the death penalty is applied discriminately toward blacks, Hispanics, Native Americans; and

WHEREAS 80 percent of the men and women on death row could not afford an attorney; and

WHEREAS executions have been recently resumed in Florida; and

WHEREAS we are concerned about possible executions of hundreds of persons in this nation over the next few years; therefore

BE IT RESOLVED that the Twelfth General Synod of the United Church of Christ reaffirm opposition to the death penalty, and that it call upon its brother-in-Christ and United Church of Christ member, the governor of Florida, to cease the authorization of additional executions in Florida, and further call upon governors of all states to refrain from authorization of executions;

BE IT FURTHER RESOLVED that the Twelfth General Synod instruct its president to continue to try to communicate directly with the governor of Florida on its behalf expressing deep pastoral concern and moral anguish over the governor's role in inspiring the resumption of executions in this country; and

BE IT FURTHER RESOLVED that all General Synod delegates and visitors from those states wherein the death penalty currently exists be encouraged to petition their governors and state legislators to reconsider and review those existing statutes which legalize the killing of human beings; and

BE IT ALSO FURTHER RESOLVED that the Twelfth General Synod recognize the failure of the church to affect the moral climate of this nation on this matter where polls indicate a majority of the people both endorse and support capital punishment and that it enable its instrumentalities and agencies to develop additional resources needed to educate and organize the UCC constituency on this issue; and the conferences be encouraged to assist local churches and individual members of the United Church of Christ to engage in serious ethical reflection and prayer-guided action toward eradication of legalized execution and the creation of a more just and humane society. We will continue to offer our prayers on behalf of our brother-in-Christ, and our brothers and sisters on death row in hopes we may end further legalized killing.

—*Resolution of the 12th General Synod of the United Church of Christ, 1979.*

Selected International Statements on the Death Penalty[1]

American Convention on Human Rights [Extract]

Article 4. Right to life.

1. Every person has the right to have his life respected. This right shall be protected by law, and, in general, from the moment of conception. No one shall be arbitrarily deprived of life.

2. In countries that have not abolished the death penalty, this may be imposed only for the most serious crimes and pursuant to a final judgment rendered by a competent court and in accordance with the law establishing such punishment, enacted prior to the commission of the crime. Its application shall not be extended to crimes to which it does not presently apply.

3. The death penalty shall not be reestablished in states that have abolished it.

4. In no case shall capital punishment be inflicted for political offenses or related common crimes.

5. Capital punishment shall not be imposed upon persons who, at the time the crime was committed, were under 18 years of age or over 70 years of age; nor shall it be applied to pregnant women.

6. Every person condemned to death shall have the right to apply for amnesty, pardon, or commutation of sentence, which may be granted in all cases. Capital punishment shall not be imposed while such a petition is pending a decision by the competent authority.

Council of Europe [Extract]

Protocol No. 6 to the Convention for the Protection of Human Rights and Fundamental Freedoms [European Convention on Human Rights] concerning the abolition of the death penalty.

The member States of the Council of Europe, signatory to this Protocol to the Convention for the Protection of Human Rights and Fundamental Freedoms, signed at Rome on 4 November 1950 (hereafter referred to as "the Convention").

Considering that the evolution that has occurred in several member States of the Council of Europe expresses a general tendency in favor of abolition of the death penalty;

Have agreed as follows:

Article 1. The penalty of death shall be abolished. No one shall be condemned to such penalty or executed.

Article 2. A State may make provision in its law for the death penalty in respect to acts committed in time of war or of imminent threat of war; such penalty shall be applied only in the instances laid down by law and in accordance with its provisions. The State shall communicate to the Secretary General of the Council of Europe the relevant provisions of the law.

The European Parliament

Resolution on the Abolition of the Death Penalty and the accession to the Sixth Protocol to the Convention for the Protection of Human Rights and Fundamental Freedoms, adopted by the European Parliament on 17 January 1986. [Extract]

A. Recalling its resolution of 18 June 1981 on the abolition of the death penalty in the European Community in which it expressed its "strong desire that the death penalty should be abolished throughout the Community" and invited Member States to amend their legal provisions, where necessary, and to take active steps within the Committee of Ministers of the Council of Europe to ensure that the European Convention on Human Rights is amended accordingly.

B. Whereas the death penalty is a cruel and inhuman form of punishment and a violation of the right to life, even where strict legal procedures are applied. . . .

Organization of the American States

Protocol to the American Convention on Human Rights to Abolish the Death Penalty. Adopted by the General Assembly of the Organization of American States at its 20th Regular Session on 8 June 1990 in Ascunsión, Paraguay.

The States Parties to this Protocol, Considering:

That Article 4 of the American Convention on Human Rights recognizes the right to life and restricts the application of the death penalty;

That everyone has the inalienable right to the respect for his life, a right that cannot be suspended for any reason;

That the tendency among the American States is to be in favor of the abolition of the death penalty;

That the application of the death penalty has irrevocable consequences, forecloses the correction of judicial error, and precludes any possibility of changing or rehabilitating those convicted;

That the abolition of the death penalty helps to insure more effective protection of the right to life;

That an international agreement must be arrived at that will entail a progressive development of the American Convention on Human Rights, and

That State Parties to the American Convention on Human Rights have expressed their intention to adopt an international agreement with a view to consolidating the practice of not applying the death penalty in the Americas,

Have agreed to sign the following Protocol to the American Convention on Human Rights to Abolish the Death Penalty.

Article 1

The States Parties to this Protocol shall not apply the death penalty in their territory to any person subject to their jurisdiction.

Article 2

1. No reservations may be made to this Protocol. However, at the time of ratification or accession, the States Parties to this instrument may declare that they reserve the right to apply the death penalty in wartime in accordance with international law, for extremely serious crimes of a military nature.

2. The State Party making this reservation shall, upon ratification or accession, inform the Secretary General of the Organization of American States of the pertinent provisions of its national legislation applicable in wartime, as referred to in the preceding paragraph.

3. Said State Party shall notify the Secretary General of the Organization of American States of the beginning or end of any state of war in effect in its territory.

Article 3

This Protocol shall be open for signature and ratification or accession by any State Party to the American Convention on Human Rights.

Ratification of this Protocol or accession thereto shall be made through the deposit of an instrument of ratification or accession with the General Secretariat of the Organization of American States.

Article 4

This Protocol shall enter into force among the States that ratify or accede to it when they deposit their respective instruments of ratification or accession with the General Secretariat of the Organization of American States.

United Nations

General Assembly Resolution 32/61 of December 8, 1977 [Extract]

Having regard to Article 3 of the universal Declaration of Human Rights, which affirms everyone's right to life and Article 6 of the international Covenant on Civil and Political Rights, which also affirms the right to life as inherent to every human being. . . .

1. *Reaffirms* that, as established by the General Assembly in resolution 2857 (XXVI) and by the Economic and Social Council in resolutions 1574 (L), 1745 (LIV), and 1930 (LVIII), the main objective to be pursued in the field of capital punishment is that of progressively restricting the number of offenses for which the death penalty may be imposed with a view to the desirability of abolishing this punishment.

Congress of Non-Governmental Organizations

Sixth United Nations Congress on the Prevention of Crime and the Treatment of Offenders, Caracas, Venezuela, 25 August to 5 September, 1980. A joint statement by 42 International Non-Governmental Organizations Concerned with Human Rights in Consultative Status with the Economic and Social Council. [Extract]

The Undersigned International Non-Governmental Organizations Concerned with Human Rights,

Affirming their unswerving commitment to the protection of the right to life of every human being,

Reiterating their total opposition to any form of cruel, inhuman, or degrading treatment or punishment,

Considering that the death penalty is in violation of both the above principles,

1. Call on all governments that retain capital punishment to cease employing it;

2. Call on the General Assembly of the United Nations to promulgate a declaration that would urge its total worldwide abolition;

3. Call on all nongovernmental organizations concerned with human rights to make every effort at the national and international level to secure the abolition of capital punishment.

Amnesty International
Anti-Slavery Society
Arab Lawyers Union
Caritas Internationalis
Commission of the Churches on International Affairs of the World Council of Churches
Friends World Committee for Consultation (Quakers)
International Alliance of Women
International Association for Religious Freedom
International Association of Democratic Lawyers
International Confederation of Free Trade Unions
International Council of Jewish Women
International Federation of Free Journalists
International Federation of Human Rights
International Federation of Women Lawyers
International League for Human Rights
International Movement for Fraternal Union Among Races and Peoples
International Organization—Justice and Development
International Peace Bureau
International Social Service
International Union for Child Welfare

International Union of Judges
International Young Christian Workers
International Youth and Student Movement for the United Nations
Minority Rights Group
Pax Christi
Pax Romana
Socialist International Women
Societe Internationale de Prophylaxie Criminelle
Union of Arab Jurists
War Resisters International
Women's International League for Peace and Freedom
Women's International Zionist Organization
World Alliance of Young Men's Christians Associations
World Assembly of Youth
World Confederation of Labor
World Federation of United Nations Associations
World Jewish Congress
World Muslim Congress
World Student Christian Federation
World Union of Catholic Women's Organizations
World Young Women's Christian Associations

Quotes on the Death Penalty[1]

Samuel Johnson, writing against the use of the death penalty for thieves:

The learned, the judicious, the pious Boerhaave relates, that he never saw a criminal dragged to execution without asking himself, "Who knows whether this man is not less culpable than me?" On the days when the prisons of this city are emptied into the grave, let every spectator of the dreadful procession put the same question to his own heart. Few among those that crowd in thousands to the legal massacre, and look with carelessness, perhaps with triumph, on the utmost exacerbations of human misery, would then be able to return without horror and dejection. —*Rambler, no. 114 (1751)*. [Montagu]

Oliver Goldsmith, writing against the use of the death penalty for thieves:

Our Saxon ancestors, fierce as they were in war, had but few executions in times of peace; and in all commencing governments that have the print of nature still strong upon them, scarce any crime is held capital.

It is among the citizens of a refined community, that penal laws, which are in the hands of the rich, are laid upon the poor. Government, while it grows older, seems to acquire the moroseness of age: and , as if our property were to become dearer in proportion as it increased; as if the more enormous our wealth, the more extensive our fears; all our possessions are paled up with new edicts every day, and hung round with gibbets to scare every invader. —*1760*. [Montagu]

Attributed to Voltaire:

It hath long since been observed, that a man after he is hanged is good for nothing, and that punishment invented for the good of society, ought to be useful to society. It is evident, that a score of stout robbers, condemned for life to some public work, would serve the state in their punishment, and that hanging them is a benefit to nobody but the executioner.—*Commentary on Cesare Beccaria, c. 1770*. [Greenhaven]

Benjamin Franklin, writing against the use of the death penalty for thieves:

If I am not myself so barbarous, so bloody-minded, and revengeful, as to kill a fellow creature for stealing from me fourteen shillings, and three pence, how can I approve of a law that does it?
—*Letter to Benjamin Vaughan, 1785*. [Montagu]

Jeremy Bentham:

The infliction of this punishment originated in resentment, indulging itself in rigor; and in sloth, which, in rapid destruction of offenders, found the great advantage of avoiding all thought. Death! always death! this requires neither the exertion of reason, nor the subjugation of passion.

If the legislator be desirous to inspire humanity amongst the citizens, let him set the example; let him show the utmost respect not only for the life of man, but for every circumstance by which the sensibility can be influenced. Sanguinary laws have a tendency to render men cruel, either by fear, by imitation, or by revenge. But laws dictated by mildness humanize the manners of a nation and the spirit of government. —*Traits of Legislation.* [Montagu]

Percy Bysshe Shelley:
    The first law which it becomes a reformer to propose and support, at the approach of a period of great political change, is the abolition of the punishment of death. It is sufficiently clear that revenge, retaliation, atonement, expiation, are rules and motives so far from deserving a place in any enlightened system of political life that they are the chief sources of a prodigious class of miseries in the domestic circles of society.
—*Essay on the Punishment of Death, published 1852.* [McGehee]

Victor Hugo:
    The man has a family; and then do you think the fatal stroke wounds him alone?—that his father, his mother, or his children will not suffer by it? In killing him, you vitally injure all his family; and thus again you punish the innocent. —*The Last Days of the Condemned, 1840.* [McGehee]

Horace Greeley:
    Man has a natural horror of taking the life of his fellow man. His instincts revolt at it—his conscience condemns it—his frame shudders at the thought of it. But let him see first one and then another strung up between heaven and earth and choked to death, with due formalities of Law and solemnities of Religion—the slayer not accounted an evil-doer but an executor of the State's just decree, a pillar of the Social edifice—and his horror of bloodshed *per se* sensibly and rapidly oozes away, and he comes to look at killing men as quite the thing provided there be adequate reason for it.
—*Hints Toward Reform in Lectures, Addresses and Other Writings, 1850.* [Greenhaven]

Unknown person quoted by Havelock Ellis:
    [Capital punishment is] the shameful practice of hiring for a guinea an assassin to accomplish a sentence which the judge would not have the courage to carry out himself. [McGehee]

William Randolph Hearst:
    Cruelty and viciousness are not abolished by cruelty and viciousness—not even legalized cruelty and viciousness. . . . We cannot cure murder by

murder. We must adopt another and better system.
—*The Congressional Digest, August- September, 1927.* [Greenhaven]

Clarence Darrow:
Even now, are not all imaginative and humane people shocked at the spectacle of a killing by the state? How many men and women would be willing to act as executioners? How many fathers and mothers would want their children to witness official killing? What kind of people read the sensational reports of an execution? If all right-thinking men and women were not ashamed of it, why would it be needful that judges and lawyers and preachers apologize for the barbarity? How can the state censure the cruelty of the man, who—moved by strong passions, or acting to save his freedom, or influenced by weakness or fear—takes human life, when everyone knows that the state itself, after long premeditation and settled hatred, not only kills, but first tortures and bedevils its victims for weeks with the impending doom?—*"The Futility of the Death Penalty,"* The Forum, *September 1928.* [Greenhaven]

Will Rogers:
Anybody whose pleasure is watching somebody else die is about as little use to humanity as the person being electrocuted. There is some excuse for the man being electrocuted. He may be innocent, he may have killed in a wild rage of passion, or not be in his right mind, or [acted in] self-defense. But the people who asked to come there just for the outing—there is no excuse in the world for them. I believe that I could stand to be the victim rather than to see one. I bet if the warden did turn the juice on these spectators, any jury in the world would set him free. —*The Autobiography of Will Rogers, 1949.* [McGehee]

Aldous Huxley:
When public executions were abolished, it was not because the majority desired their abolition; it was because a small minority of exceptionally sensitive reformers possessed sufficient influence to have them banned. In one of its aspects, civilization may be defined as a systematic withholding from individuals of certain occasions for barbarous behavior.
—*The Devils of Loudun, 1952.* [McGehee]

Arthur Koestler:
There is also a larger issue involved, for the gallows is not merely a machine of death, but the oldest and most obscene symbol of that tendency in mankind which drives it towards moral self-destruction.
—*Reflections on Hanging, 1957.* [McGehee]

Albert Camus
If, therefore, there is a desire to maintain the death penalty, let us at least be spared the hypocrisy of a justification by example. Let us be frank about the

penalty which can have no publicity, that intimidation which works only on respectable people, so long as they are respectable, which fascinates those who have ceased to be respectable and debases or deranges those who take part in it. It is a penalty, to be sure, a frightful torture, both physical and moral, and it provides no sure example except a demoralizing one. It punishes, but it forestalls nothing; indeed, it may even arouse the impulse to murder. It hardly seems to exist, except for the man who suffers it—in his soul for months and years, in his body during the desperate and violent hour when he is cut in two without suppressing his life. Let us call it by the name which, for lack of any other nobility, will at least give the nobility of truth, and let us recognize it for what it is essentially: a revenge.[2]

National Death Penalty Abolitionist Groups

Amnesty International
Program to Abolish the
Death Penalty
322 Eighth Avenue
New York, NY 10001-4808
212-807-8400
FAX 212-627-1451
http://www.amnesty.org/ailib/
intcam/dp/

Capital Punishment Project
American Civil Liberties Union
122 Maryland Avenue NE
Washington, DC 20002
202-675-2321
FAX 202-546-0738

The Death Penalty Information
Center
1320 18th Street, NW, 5th Floor
Washington, DC 20036
202-293-6970
Fax: 202-822-4787
http://www.essential.org/dpic

Murder Victims Families
for Reconciliation
PO Box 208
Atlantic, VA 23303-0208
804-824-0948

NAACP Legal Defense and
Educational Fund, Inc.
Suite 1600
99 Hudson Street
New York, NY 10013-2897
212-219-1900
FAX 212-226-7592

National Coalition to Abolish the
Death Penalty
918 F Street NW, Suite 601
Washington, DC 20004
202-387-3890

Notes

Chapter 1. Life for Life: Old Testament Perspectives

1. *The Interpreter's Bible*, vol. 1 (New York: Abingdon Press, 1951), pp. 999-1000.

2. Howard Zehr, *Death as a Penalty* (Elkhart, Ind.: MCC U.S. Office of Criminal Justice, 1987), p. 18.

3. Rene A. Wormser, *The Story of the Law and the Men Who Made It from Earliest Times to the Present* (New York: Simon and Schuster, 1962), pp. 26-27.

4. Since the death penalty was reinstated in the case of Gregg versus Georgia, attempts have been made to make its application consistent and fair. However, while making the death penalty process exceedingly complicated, court decisions made since Gregg v. Georgia have shown the judicial system's inability to treat capital cases in a consistent manner. A book-length study that shows the inconsistency of the application of the death penalty in Florida is provided in Dave Von Drehle, *Among the Lowest of the Dead: The Culture of Death Row* (New York: Random House, 1995).

5. "Capital Punishment," *BJS Bulletin*, Sept. 1991.

6. *BJS National Update* (Oct. 1991), p. 4.

7. [There are] "an estimated 250 individuals with mental retardation on death row nationwide," says J. H. Blume, "Representing the Mentally Retarded Defendant," *The Champion* 32:34-38 (Nov. 1987), quoted in Nolene B. Weaver, *Offenders in Idaho's Developmental Disabilities and Criminal Justice System* (Boise, Idaho: Idaho State Council on Developmental Disabilities, 1988), p. 15. "Currently more than 300 persons with mental retardation have been identified on death row throughout the United States. It is likely that many more inmates with permanent mental deficiencies have gone undetected through both trial and sentencing": *Questions and Answers on Mental Retardation and the Death Penalty* (Washington, D.C.: National Coalition to Abolish the

Death Penalty, 1990), p. 2.

8. Carolyn Callahan and Michael DiLeo, "Capital Crime: Notes on the Death Penalty," *Mother Jones* (Sept. 1989).

9. In McCleskey v. Kemp 481 U.S. 279, the United States Supreme Court accepted data that revealed prosecutors sought the death penalty in 70 percent of the cases where black defendants killed white people but only 19 percent of the cases where white defendants were accused of murdering black victims. The majority opinion which upheld the death penalty described these disparities as "an inevitable part of our criminal justice system." Quoted in *Chattahoochee Judicial District, Buckle of the Black Belt: The Death Penalty in Microcosm* (Washington, D.C.: Death Penalty Information Center, 1991), p. 2.

10. Stuart Taylor, "Small Errors Do Not Require Reversal in Death Sentences," *New York Times* (June 1, 1988), p. A26. In a dissenting opinion, Justice Thurgood Marshall stated, "The speculation engendered by harmless error . . . in the context of a capital sentencing proceeding presents an intolerable danger that the death sentence will be administered erroneously."

11. Howard Zehr, "MCC Commentary: Executing the Innocent —U.S. v. Biblical Justice," *Lifelines*, no. 59 (Jan.-Mar. 1993), pp. 3ff.

Chapter 2. One Without Sin: New Testament Perspectives

1. *The Interpreter's Bible*, vol. 7 (New York: Abingdon Press, 1952), p. 586.

2. Marshall Frady, "Death in Arkansas," *The New Yorker* (Feb. 22, 1993), pp. 105-133.

3. John Howard Yoder, "A Christian Perspective," in Hugo Adam Bedau, *The Death Penalty in America* (New York: Oxford University Press, 1982), p. 373.

Chapter 3. Opposition to the Death Penalty to 1700

1. Quoted in Roland H. Bainton, *Early Christianity* (Melbourne, Fla.: Robert E. Krieger Publishing, 1960) p. 151.

2. Roland H. Bainton, *Christian Attitudes Toward War and Peace* (Nashville: Abingdon, 1960), p. 78.

3. Ibid., p. 71.

4. Rene A. Wormser, *The Story of Law and the Men Who Made It— From Earliest Times to the Present* (New York: Simon and Schuster, 1962), p. 177.

5. St. Augustine, *The City of God* (New York: The Modern Library, 1950), p. 27.

6. Bainton, *Early Christianity*, p. 82.

7. John Laurence, *A History of Capital Punishment* (Port Washington, N.Y.: Kennikat Press, 1971), pp. 6-7.

8. Ibid., p. 4.

9. Thieleman J. van Braght, *The Bloody Theater or Martyrs Mirror of the Defenseless Christians* (Scottdale, Pa.: Herald Press, 1987), p. 282.

10. *The Schleitheim Confession*, trans. and ed. John Howard Yoder (Scottdale, Pa.: Herald Press, 1973), p. 14.

11. Van Braght, p. 1131.

12. Quoted in Basil Montagu (ed.), *The Opinions of Different Authors upon the Punishment of Death* (London: Longman, Hurst, Rees, and Paternoster Row, 1809; reprinted Buffalo, N.Y.: William S. Hein & Company, 1984), p. 59.

13. Ibid., p. 52.

Chapter 4. Modern Opposition to the Death Penalty

1. John Laurence, *A History of Capital Punishment* (Port Washington, N.Y.: Kennikat Press, 1971), p. 13.

2. Ibid., p. 18.

3. *Three Centuries of Debate on the Death Penalty*, ed. Greenhaven Staff (St. Paul, Minn.: Greenhaven Press, 1986), pp. 22-28. Quoted from Cesare Beccaria, *An Essay on Crimes and Punishments,* originally published in London by F. Newberg, 1775.

4. Fyodor Dostoyevsky, *The Idiot* (New York: Penguin Books, 1955), p. 46.

5. *Against the Death Penalty* (New Delhi, India: Amnesty International Indian Section, n.d.), p. 14.

6. *Three Centuries of Debate on the Death Penalty*, pp. 34-35.

7. From William Makepeace Thackeray, "Going to See a Man Hanged," quoted in Edward G. McGehee and William H. Hildebrand, *The Death Penalty: A Literary and Historical Approach* (Boston: D.C. Heath and Company, 1964), pp. 58-64.

8. From Charles Dickens, "Three Letters in the Daily News, for March 9, 13, and 16, 1846," ibid., pp. 107-113.

9. Laurence, pp. 14-21.

10. Information Plus, *Capital Punishment: Cruel and Unusual?* (Wylie, Tex.: Information Plus, 1994), p. 3.

11. Jan Gorecki, *Capital Punishment: Criminal Law and Social Evolution* (New York: Columbia University Press, 1983), p. 86.

12. Robert H. Loeb Jr. and George F. Cole, *Crime and Capital Punishment* (New York: Franklin Watts, 1986), pp. 30-34.

Chapter 5. Deterrence? Social and Psychological Factors Say No

1. Idaho Department of Corrections, *Volunteer Orientation Packet* (Boise: Idaho Department of Corrections, n.d.), p. 13.

2. Dorothy Otney Lewis, "Neuropsychiatric, Psychoeducational, and Family Characteristics of 14 Juveniles Condemned to Death in the United States," *American Journal of Psychiatry* 145/5 (May, 1988): 584-589.

3. Katherine Bishop, "The Man-Made Disasters on Death Row," *The New York Times* (April 8, 1990), sect. 4, p. 4.

4. According to *Statistical Abstract of the United States 1995* (Washington, D.C.: U.S. Bureau of the Census, 1995), p. 95, in 1992 African-American men were more than seven times as likely to die from homicide as were white men: 67.5 per 100,000 for blacks compared to 9.1 per 100,000 for whites. Homicide was the third leading cause of death among African-American men; the tenth leading cause of death for white men.

5. "Only a small proportion of first-degree murderers is sentenced to death, and even fewer are executed. Although death sentences since 1980 have increased in number to about 250 per year, this is still only 1 per cent of all homicides known to the police. Of all those convicted on a charge of criminal homicide, only 2 percent—about 1 in 50—are eventually sentenced to death," says Hugo Adam Bedau, *The Case Against the Death Penalty* (Washington, D.C.: American Civil Liberties Union, 1992). On-line: gopher://gopher.nyc.pipeline. com:6601/00/issues/death/case__against

6. Bureau of Justice Statistics. *Sourcebook of Criminal Justice Statistics—1991* (Washington, D.C.: U.S. Department of Justice, 1992), p. 473.

7. Ibid., p. 629.

8. *The Idaho Statesman*, July 18, 1993, p. 1C.

9. Anthony G. Amsterdam, "Capital Punishment," in Hugo Adam Bedau, *The Death Penalty in America* (New York: Oxford University Press, 1982), p. 357.

10. NAACP Legal Defense and Educational Fund, Inc. *Death Row U.S.A.* (Spring 1993), pp. 4-8.

11. Ibid., p. 1.

12. This rate was figured as follows: the total number of death row inmates held as of April 20, 1993 (2,729) was divided into 100,000, giving 36.64. This number was multiplied times the 36 suicides giving a rate of 1319.16 per 100,000 for the 21-year period between 1972 and 1993. This number was then divided by 21 to give an

annual rate of 62.82. Since this rate was figured on the current population of death row, rather than the number of inmates on death row each year, it is lower than the actual suicide rate per 100,000, if it were to be figured on an annual basis.

13. *Statistical Abstract of the United States 1992*, p. 89.

14. Stuart Sutherland, *The International Dictionary of Psychology* (New York: Continum, 1989), p. 254.

15. Dorothy Otney Lewis, "Neuropsychiatric. . . ."

16. "Testimony of James W. Ellis as President of the American Association on Mental Retardation, Before the United States Senate Committee on the Judiciary, September 27, 1989."

17. Hans J. Eysenck and Gisli H. Gudjonsson, *The Causes and Cures of Criminality* (New York: Plenum Press, 1989), p. 89.

Chapter 6. Deterrence? Statistics Say No

1. Unless otherwise noted, the information about various statistical studies in this chapter comes from an excellent historical survey of statistical approaches to the death penalty found in William J. Bowers, "The Effect of Executions Is Brutalization, Not Deterrence," in Kenneth C. Haas and James A. Inciardi, eds., *Challenging Capital Punishment: Legal and Social Science Approaches* (Newbury Park, Calif.: Sage Publications, 1988), pp. 49-89.

2. *Ibid*, p. 66.

3. Hans Zeisel, "The Deterrent Effect of the Death Penalty: Facts v. Faith," in Hugo A. Bedau, ed., *The Death Penalty in America* (New York: Oxford University Press, 1982), pp. 125-133.

4. William C. Bailey and Ruth D. Peterson, "Murder, Capital Punishment and Deterrence: A Review of the Evidence and an Examination of Police Killings," *Journal of Social Issues* (Summer 1994): 52-75.

5. In January, 1995, 386 police chiefs and sheriffs rated the death penalty as the least cost-effective way for reducing violent crime. See "Death Penalty Debate," *CQ Research* 5 (Mar. 10, 1995): 193-216.

Chapter 7. The Death Penalty and Repeat Offenders

1. Richard Dieter, *Sentencing for Life: Americans Embrace Alternatives to the Death Penalty* (Washington, D.C.: The Death Penalty Information Center, 1993), p. 5.

2. Dieter, *Sentencing for Life*, pp. 19-20.

3. Field Research Corporation, *Californians' Attitudes About the Death Penalty: Results of a Statewide Survey* (New York: Amnesty Inter-

national, 1990).

4. Cambridge Survey Research, *An Analysis of Political Attitudes Towards the Death Penalty in the State of Florida: Executive Summary* (New York: Amnesty International, 1986).

5. *Idaho Policy Survey* (Boise, Idaho: The Survey Research Center, School of Social Sciences and Public Affairs, Boise State University, 1991), pp. 26-27.

6. Urban Research Institute, University of Louisville, *Attitudes in the State of Kentucky on the Death Penalty* (New York: Amnesty International, 1989).

7. David Weissbrodt, "New Poll Shows Minnesotans Strongly Prefer Life Sentence over Death Penalty," report on a poll conducted by the University of Minnesota Center for Survey Research, Oct.-Dec. 1992. The figure for those favoring capital punishment was taken from a poll conducted by the *Minnesota Star Tribune*, Aug. 1991.

8. William J. Bowers, and Margaret Vandiver, *Nebraskans Want an Alternative to the Death Penalty: Executive Summary of a Nebraska State Survey Conducted April 26-28, 1991* (Boston: College of Criminal Justice, Northeastern University, 1991).

9. William J. Bowers and Margaret Vandiver, *New Yorkers Want an Alternative to the Death Penalty: Executive Summary of a New York State Survey Conducted March 1-4, 1991* (Boston: College of Criminal Justice, Northeastern University, 1991).

10. Cited by Information Plus, "A General History of Capital Punishment in America," in Robert M. Baird and Stuart E. Rosenbaum, *Punishment and the Death Penalty* (Amherst, N.Y.: Prometheus Books, 1994), pp. 108.

11. James W. Marquart, Sheldon Ekland-Olson, and Jonathan Sorensen, *The Rope, the Chair, and the Needle; Capital Punishment in Texas, 1923-1990* (Austin, Tex.: The University of Texas Press, 1994), pp. 123-125.

12. Ibid., pp. 125-126.

13. Ibid., pp. 182-183.

14. Ibid., pp. 183-184.

Chapter 8. What About the Victims?

1. "Church's Killer Pleads Guilty," *The Denver Post* (May 25, 1995), p. 1.

2. Pelke's and Jaeger's stories are told in *Murder Close Up*, a videotape by the Mennonite Board of Missions (Harrisonburg, Va.: Mennonite Media Ministries, 1995).

3. Kathy Dillon, "Mercy, Compassion, and Forgiveness," *The Voice* (no. 5, summer 1995), p. 5.

Chapter 9. The Death Penalty and Race

1. In 1993 the murder rate for African-Americans was 33.5 per 100,000, compared to 3.9 per 100,000 for whites. Bureau of Justice Statistics, *Sourcebook of Criminal Justice Statistics, 1994* (Washington, D.C.: U.S. Department of Justice, 1995), p. 342.

2. Brandon S. Centerwall, "Race, Socioeconomic Status, and Domestic Homicide," *JAMA, The Journal of the American Medical Association* 273/22 (June 14, 1995): 1755 (4).

3. *Statistical Abstract of the United States 1995* (Washington, D.C.: U.S. Department of Commerce, 1995), p. 484.

4. U.S. Department of Labor, *Monthly Labor Review* 119/5 (May 1996): 62.

5. *Death Penalty Legislation and the Racial Justice Act: Hearings Before the Subcommittee on Civil and Constitutional Rights of the Committee on the Judiciary House of Representatives, 101st Congress, Second Session, on H.R. 4618: Racial Justice Act of 1990* (Washington, D.C.: U.S. Government Printing Office, 1991), p. 91.

6. Bureau of Justice Statistics, *Sourcebook, 1994,* p. 338.

7. NAACP Legal Defense and Educational Fund, Capital Punishment Project. *Death Row, U.S.A.* (April 30, 1995).

8. *Uniform Crime Reports for the United States 1994* (Washington, D.C.: Federal Bureau of Investigation, 1995), p. 14.

9. Ibid.

10. *Death Penalty Legislation and the Racial Justice Act,* p. 69.

11. Ibid., p. 70.

12. Ibid., pp. 156-166.

13. Ibid., p. 115.

Chapter 10. The Death Penalty and the Mentally Retarded

1. Herbert J. Grossman, ed., *Classification in Mental Retardation.* (Washington, D.C.: American Association on Mental Retardation, 1983), cited in "Testimony of James W. Ellis as President of the American Association on Mental Retardation, Before the United States Senate Committee on the Judiciary, September 27, 1989."

2. [There are] "an estimated 250 individuals with mental retardation on death row nationwide," says J. H. Blume, "Representing the Mentally Retarded Defendant," *The Champion* 32 (Nov. 1987): 34-38, quoted in Nolene B. Weaver, *Offenders in Idaho's Developmental Disabili-*

ties and Criminal Justice System (Boise, Idaho: Idaho State Council on Developmental Disabilities, 1988), p. 15. "Currently more than 300 persons with mental retardation have been identified on death row throughout the United States. It is likely that many more inmates with permanent mental deficiencies have gone undetected through both trial and sentencing": *Questions and Answers on: Mental Retardation and the Death Penalty* (Washington, D.C.: National Coalition to Abolish the Death Penalty, 1990), p. 2.

3. James W. Ellis and Ruth W. Luckasson, "Mentally Retarded Criminal Defendants," *George Washington Law Review* 53 (1985): 414-492.

4. Ibid.

5. Weaver, *Offenders,* pp. 19-20.

6. Ellis and Luckasson, "Mentally Retarded," p. 430.

7. Patricia Smith, "The Execution of Jerome Bowden: 'Bringing to Light Something Wrong,' " *The Atlantic Constitution,* June 28, 1986.

8. Ibid.

9. Field Research Corporation, *Californians' Attitudes About the Death Penalty: Results of a Statewide Survey* (New York: Amnesty International, 1990).

10. Cambridge Survey Research, *An Analysis of Political Attitudes Towards the Death Penalty in the State of Florida: Executive Summary* (New York: Amnesty International, 1986).

11. Urban Research Institute, University of Louisville, *Attitudes in the State of Kentucky on the Death Penalty* (New York: Amnesty International, 1989).

12. William J. Bowers and Margaret Vandiver, *New Yorkers Want an Alternative to the Death Penalty: Executive Summary of a New York State Survey Conducted March 1-4, 1991* (Boston: College of Criminal Justice, Northeastern University, 1991).

13. Princeton Survey Research Associates *Newsweek* Poll (July 1995).

14. Ellis, "Testimony."

Chapter 11. Capital punishment—for People with No Capital
1. Hugo Adam Bedau, *The Case Against the Death Penalty* (Washington, DC: American Civil Liberties Union, 1992). On-line: gopher://gopher.nyc.pipeline.com: 6601/00/issues/death/case__against

2. Carolyn Callahan and Michael DiLeo, "Capital Crime: Notes on the Death Penalty," *Mother Jones,* Sept. 1989.

3. Stephen B. Bright, "Counsel for the Poor: The Death Sentence Not for the Worst Crime But for the Worst Lawyer," *Yale Law Journal* 103 (1994): 1835-1883.

4. Ibid.

5. Bureau of Justice Statistics, *Sourcebook of Criminal Justice Statistics—1991* (Washington, D.C.: U.S. Department of Justice, 1992), p. 214.

6. Bedau, *The Case Against the Death Penalty.*

Chapter 12. The Innocent Have Been Executed

1. Michael L. Radelet, Hugo Adam Bedau, and Constance E. Putnam, *In Spite of Innocence: Erroneous Convictions in Capital Cases* (Boston: Northeastern University Press, 1992).

2. A book-length review of this case can be found in Nick Davies, *White Lies: Rape Murder and Justice Texas Style* (New York: Pantheon Books, 1991).

3. Information about the Abu-Jamal case comes from E. L. Doctorow, "From Here to Death Row," *New York Times,* July 14, 1995, p. 25; Salim Muwakkil, "Politics, Revenge Power Death Penalty Case," *Chicago Sun-Times,* June 24, 1995, p. 23; and Don Terry, "New Witness Comes Forward Saying Journalist Is Not Killer," *New York Times,* Aug. 11, 1995, p. A14.

4. Howard Zehr, "MCC Commentary: Executing the Innocent—U.S. v. Biblical Justice," *Lifelines,* no. 59 (Jan.-Mar. 1993), p. 5.

5. John Flannery, "With Liberty and Justice for All?" *The Champion,* Apr. 1995, pp. 35ff.

Chapter 13. The Cost of Death

1. Richard C. Dieter, *Millions Misspent: What Politicians Don't Say About the High Costs of the Death Penalty* (Washington, D.C.: Death Penalty Information Center, 1993), p. 3.

2. *Capital Losses: The Price of the Death Penalty for New York State; A Report from the Public Defense Backup Center to the Senate Finance Committee, the Assembly Ways and Means Committee and the Division of the Budget* (Albany, N.Y.: New York State Defenders Association, Inc., 1982), p. 13.

3. Ibid., p. 3.

4. Ibid.

5. Cited by the Kansas Legislative Research Department in "Memorandum: Costs of Implementing the Death Penalty—H.B. 2062 as Amended by the House Committee of the Whole," unpublished report.

6. A Kansas Legislative Research Department study, cited in Dieter, *Millions Misspent*, p. 3.

7. *Capital Losses*, p. 7.

8. *Atlanta Constitution*, February 11, 1982, p. 1. Cited in *Capital Losses*.

9. A New York Department of Corrections study cited in Dieter, *Millions Misspent*, p. 3.

10. Kansas Legislative Research Department, p. 7.

11. Michael L. Radelet, Hugo Adam Bedau, and Constance E. Putnam, *In Spite of Innocence: Erroneous Convictions in Capital Cases* (Boston: Northeastern University Press, 1992).

Chapter 14. The Effects on Society

1. Robert Reinhold, "24 Minutes to Deadline," *New York Times*, Oct. 6, 1983, p. A29.

2. Scott Wesely, "As Otey Executed, 'All Our Souls Are Diminished,' " *Nebraskans Against the Death Penalty Newsletter*, Sept. 1994, p. 1.

3. Victor Streib, *The Juvenile Death Penalty Today: Present Death Row Inmates Under Juvenile Death Sentences and Death Sentences and Executions for Juvenile Crimes, January 1, 1973, to May 1, 1991* (Cleveland, Ohio: Cleveland-Marshall College of Law, 1991), pp. 2, 5-8.

4. Field Research Corporation, *Californians' Attitudes About the Death Penalty: Results of a Statewide Survey* (New York: Amnesty International, 1990).

5. Cambridge Survey Research, *An Analysis of Political Attitudes Towards the Death Penalty in the State of Florida: Executive Summary* (New York: Amnesty International, 1986).

6. Urban Research Institute, University of Louisville, *Attitudes in the State of Kentucky on the Death Penalty* (New York: Amnesty International, 1989).

7. Gallup Organization, *Cable News Network, USA Today Poll*, Sept. 1994.

8. Princeton Survey Research Associates *Newsweek* Poll (July 1995).

9. Marshall Frady, "Death in Arkansas," *The New Yorker*, Feb. 22, 1993, pp. 105-133.

10. *Amnesty International Report 1991* (New York: Amnesty International, 1991).

Chapter 15. Cruel and Unusual Punishment

1. Robert Reinhold, "24 Minutes to Deadline," *The New York Times,* Oct. 6, 1983, sect. 1, p. 1.

2. "Florida Execution Is Called Torture," *The New York Times,* June 1, 1990, p. D16.

3. "Convicted Killer Fights for Release; Former Death Row Inmate Hopes New Trial Will Set Her Free," *Fort Lauderdale Sun-Sentinel,* June 20, 1992, p. 1B. See also Claire Safran, "Best Friends: Woman Gets Her Best Friend out of Prison," *Good Housekeeping* 219/1 (July 1994): 40.

4. Peter Applebome, "2 Electric Jolts in Alabama Execution," *The New York Times,* July 15, 1989, sect. 1, p. 6.

5. Hugo Adam Bedau, *The Case Against the Death Penalty* (Washington, D.C.: The American Civil Liberties Union, 1992).

6. Unless otherwise noted, reports of executions in this chapter are from Michael Radelet, *Botched Executions* (New York: Amnesty International, n.d.).

Religious Statements Against the Death Penalty

1. Unless otherwise noted, statements found in this section were taken from *The Death Penalty: The Religious Community Calls for Abolition* (Washington, D.C.: National Coalition to Abolish the Death Penalty, 1988).

International Statements on the Death Penalty

1. These statements and others have been collected and distributed by Amnesty International.

Quotes on the Death Penalty

1. I gathered most of these quotes from three secondary sources: Basil Montagu, ed., *The Opinions of Different Authors Upon the Punishment of Death* (London: Longman, Hurst, Rees, and Paternoster Row, 1909, reprinted Buffalo, N.Y.: William S. Hein & Company, 1984); Edward G. McGehee and William H. Hildebrand, eds., *The Death Penalty: A Literary and Historical Approach* (Boston: D.C.: Heath and Co., 1964); and *Three Centuries of Debate on the Death Penalty,* ed. Greenhaven Staff (St. Paul, Minn.: Greenhaven Press, 1986). I have indicated the secondary source for a quote by placing in square brackets following the quotes either Montagu, McGehee, or Greenhaven.

2. Albert Camus, "Reflections on the Guillotine," in *Resistance, Rebellion, and Death* (New York: The Modern Library, 1960), pp. 131-179.

Bibliography

Against the Death Penalty. New Delhi, India: Amnesty International Indian Section, n.d.

Amnesty International. *United States of America: The Death Penalty.* London: Amnesty International, 1987.

Amnesty International. *When the State Kills . . . The Death Penalty: A Human Rights Issue.* New York: Amnesty International, 1989.

Amnesty International Report 1991. New York: Amnesty International, 1991.

Applebome, Peter. "2 Electric Jolts in Alabama Execution." *The New York Times,* July 15, 1989, 1-6.

Augustine, St. *The City of God.* New York: The Modern Library, 1950.

Bailey, William C., and Ruth D. Peterson. "Murder, Capital Punishment, and Deterrence: A Review of the Evidence and an Examination of Police Killings." *Journal of Social Issues* 50 (Summer 1974): 53-75.

Bainton, Roland H. *Christian Attitudes Toward War and Peace.* Nashville: Abingdon, 1960.

_____. *Early Christianity.* Melbourne, Fla.: Robert E. Krieger Publishing, 1960.

Baird, Robert M., and Stuart E. Rosenbaum, eds. *Punishment and the Death Penalty: The Current Debate.* Amhearst, N.Y.: Prometheus Books, 1995.

Beccaria, Cesare. *On Crimes and Punishments and Other Writings.* Ed. Richard Bellamy. Texts in the History of Political Thought Series. Cambridge: Cambridge Univ. Press, 1995.

Bedau, Hugo Adam. *The Case Against the Death Penalty,* Washington, D.C.: American Civil Liberties Union, 1992.

Bedau, Hugo Adam, ed. *The Death Penalty in America.* New York: Oxford University Press, 1982.

Bishop, Katherine. "The Man-Made Disasters on Death Row." *The New York Times*, April 8, 1990, sect. 4, p. 4.

Blume, J. H. "Representing the Mentally Retarded Defendant." *The Champion* 32 (Nov. 1987): 34-38.

Bowers, William J., and Margaret Vandiver. *Nebraskans Want an Alternative to the Death Penalty: Executive Summary of a Nebraska State Survey Conducted April 26-28, 1991*. Boston: College of Criminal Justice, Northeastern University, 1991.

——————. *New Yorkers Want an Alternative to the Death Penalty: Executive Summary of a New York State Survey Conducted March 1-4, 1991*. Boston: College of Criminal Justice, Northeastern University, 1991.

Bright, Stephen B. "Counsel for the Poor: The Death Sentence Not for the Worst Crime but for the Worst Lawyer." *Yale Law Journal* 103 (1994): 1835-1883.

Bureau of Justice Statistics. *BJS National Update*, Oct. 1991.

——————. "Capital Punishment." *BJS Bulletin*, Sept. 1991.

——————. *Sourcebook of Criminal Justice Statistics—1991*. Washington, D.C.: U.S. Department of Justice, 1992.

——————. *Sourcebook of Criminal Justice Statistics, 1994*. Washington, D.C.: U.S. Department of Justice, 1995.

Callahan, Carolyn, and Michael DiLeo. "Capital Crime: Notes on the Death Penalty." *Mother Jones*, Sept. 1989.

Cambridge Survey Research. *An Analysis of Political Attitudes Towards the Death Penalty in the State of Florida: Executive Summary*. New York: Amnesty International, 1986.

Capital Losses: The Price of the Death Penalty for New York State; A Report from the Public Defense Backup Center to the Senate Finance Committee, the Assembly Ways and Means Committee and the Division of the Budget. Albany, N.Y.: New York State Defenders Association, Inc., 1982.

Centerwall, Brandon S. "Race, Socioecononmic Status, and Domestic Homicide," *JAMA, The Journal of the American Medical Association* 273/22 (June 14, 1995): 1755 (4).

Chattahoochee Judicial District, Buckle of the Black Belt: The Death Penalty in Microcosm. Washington, D.C.: Death Penalty Information Center, 1991.

"Church's Killer Pleads Guilty." *The Denver Post*, May 25, 1995, p. 1.

Clay, William L. *To Kill or Not to Kill: Thoughts on the Death Penalty.* San Bernadino, Calif.: The Borgo Press, 1990.

"Convicted Killer Fights for Release; Former Death Row Inmate Hopes New Trial Will Set Her Free." *Fort Lauderdale Sun-Sentinel*, June 20, 1992, p. 1B.

Davies, Nick. *White Lies: Rape, Murder, and Justice Texas Style.* New York: Pantheon Books, 1991.

"Death Penalty Debate." *CQ Research* 5 (Mar. 10, 1995): 193-216.

Death Penalty Legislation and the Racial Justice Act: Hearings Before the Subcommittee on Civil and Constitutional Rights of the Committee on the Judiciary House of Representatives, 101st Congress, Second Session, on H.R. 4618: Racial Justice Act of 1990. Washington, D.C.: U.S. Government Printing Office, 1991.

The Death Penalty: The Religious Community Calls for Abolition. Washington, D.C.: National Coalition to Abolish the Death Penalty, 1988.

Dieter, Richard C. *Millions Misspent: What Politicians Don't Say About the High Costs of the Death Penalty.* Washington, D.C.: Death Penalty Information Center, 1993.

_____. *Sentencing for Life: Americans Embrace Alternatives to the Death Penalty.* Washington, D.C.: The Death Penalty Information Center, 1993.

Dillon, Kathy. "Mercy, Compassion, and Forgiveness." *The Voice*, Summer 1995, 5.

Doctorow, E. L., "From Here to Death Row." *New York Times*, July 14, 1995, p. 25.

Dostoyevsky, Fyodor. *The Idiot.* New York: Penguin Books, 1955.

The Economist Book of Vital World Statistics. New York: Random House, 1991.

Ellis, James W. "Testimony as President of the American Association on Mental Retardation, Before the United States Senate Committee on the Judiciary, September 27, 1989."

Ellis, James W., and Ruth W. Luckasson. "Mentally Retarded Criminal Defendants." *George Washington Law Review* 53 (1985): 414-492.

Evangelical Lutheran Church in America. *A Statement on the Death Penalty.* Chicago: Evangelical Lutheran Church in America, 1991. On-line: http://www.elca.org/D.C.s/death.html

Eysenck, Hans J., and Gisli H. Gudjonsson. *The Causes and Cures of Criminality.* New York: Plenum Press, 1989.

Flannery, John. "With Liberty and Justice for All?" *The Champion*, April 1995, p. 35.

Field Research Corporation. *Californians' Attitudes About the Death Penalty: Results of a Statewide Survey.* New York: Amnesty International, 1990.

"Florida Execution Is Called Torture." *The New York Times*, June 1, 1990, p. D16.

Frady, Marshall. "Death in Arkansas." *The New Yorker*, Feb. 22, 1993, pp. 105-133.

Gallup Organization. *Cable News Network, U.S.A. Today Poll*, September 1994.

Gorecki, Jan. *Capital Punishment: Criminal Law and Social Evolution.* New York: Columbia University Press, 1983.

Grossman, Herbert J., ed. *Classification in Mental Retardation.* Washington, D.C.: American Association on Mental Retardation, 1983.

Haas, Kenneth C., and James A. Inciardi, eds. *Challenging Capital Punishment: Legal and Social Science Applications.* Newbury Park, Calif.: Sage Publications, 1988.

Idaho Department of Corrections. *Volunteer Orientation Packet.* Boise, Idaho: Idaho Department of Corrections, n.d.

Idaho Policy Survey. Boise, Idaho: The Survey Research Center, School of Social Sciences and Public Affairs, Boise State University, 1991.

The Idaho Statesman. July 18, 1993, p. 1C.

Information Plus. *Capital Punishment: Cruel and Unusual?* Wylie, Tex.: Information Plus, 1994.

The Interpreter's Bible. Vols. 1, 7. New York: Abingdon Press, 1951-52.

Laurence, John. *A History of Capital Punishment.* Port Washington, N.Y.: Kennikat Press, 1971.

Lawson, Edward. *Encyclopedia of Human Rights.* New York: Taylor and Davis, 1991.

Lewis, Dorothy Otney. "Neuropsychiatric, Psychoeducational, and Family Characteristics of 14 Juveniles Condemned to Death in the United States." *American Journal of Psychiatry* 145/5 (May 1988): 584-589.

Loeb, Robert H. Jr., and George F. Cole. *Crime and Capital Punishment.* New York: Franklin Watts, 1986.

Marquart, James W., Sheldon Ekland-Olsen, and Jonathan R. Sorensen. *The Rope, the Chair, and the Needle: Capital Punishment in Texas, 1923-1990.* Austin, Tex.: University of Texas Press, 1994.

Marsh, Frank H., and Janet Katz, eds. *Biology, Crime and Ethics: A Study of Biological Explanations for Criminal Behavior.* Cincinnati, Ohio: Anderson Publishing, 1985.

McGehee, Edward G., and William H. Hildebrand. *The Death Penalty: A Literary and Historical Approach.* Boston: D.C. Heath and Co., 1964.

Megivern, James J. *The Death Penalty: An Historical and Theological Survey.* Mahwah, N.J.: Paulist Press, 1997.

Mennonite Board of Missions. *Murder Close Up.* Videotape. Harrisonburg, Va.: Mennonite Media Ministries, 1995.

Montagu, Basil, ed. *The Opinions of Different Authors upon the Punishment of Death.* London: Longman, Hurst, Rees, and Paternoster Row, 1809; reprinted Buffalo, N.Y.: William S. Hein & Co., 1984.

Muwakkil, Salim. "Politics, Revenge Power Death Penalty Case." *Chicago Sun-Times,* June 24, 1995.

NAACP Legal Defense and Educational Fund, Inc. *Death Row U.S.A.* Spring 1993.

_____. Capital Punishment Project. *Death Row, U.S.A.* April 30, 1995.

"Poll: Police Chiefs Say Death Penalty Ineffective." *Associated Press,* Feb. 23, 1995.

Prejean, Helen. *Dead Man Walking: An Eyewitness Account of the Death Penalty in the United States.* New York: Random House, 1993.

Princeton Survey Research Associates *Newsweek* Poll. July 1995.

Questions and Answers on Mental Retardation and the Death Penalty. Washington, D.C.: National Coalition to Abolish the Death Penalty, 1990.

Radelet, Michael L., "Botched Executions." New York: Amnesty International, n.d.

Radelet, Michael L., Hugo Adam Bedau, and Constance E. Putnam. *In Spite of Innocence: Erroneous Convictions in Capital Cases.* Boston: Northeastern University Press, 1992.

Reinhold, Robert. "24 Minutes to Deadline." *The New York Times,* Oct. 6, 1983, sect. 1, p. 1.

Safran, Claire. "Best Friends: Woman Gets Her Best Friend out of Prison," *Good Housekeeping* 219/1 (July 1994): 40.

The Schleitheim Confession. Trans. and ed. John Howard Yoder. Scottdale, Pa.: Herald Press, 1973.

Scott, George Ryley. *The History of Capital Punishment; Including an Examination of the Case for and Against the Death Penalty.* London: Torchstream Press, 1950.

Shin, Kilman. *Death Penalty and Crime.* Fairfax, Va.: Center for Economic Analysis, George Mason University, 1978.

Smith, Patricia. "The Execution of Jerome Bowden: 'Bringing to Light Something Wrong.' " *The Atlantic Constitution,* June 28, 1986.

Statistical Abstract of the United States 1992. Washington, D.C.: Department of Commerce, 1992.

Statistical Abstract of the United States 1995. Washington, D.C.: U.S. Department of Commerce, 1995.

Streib, Victor. *The Juvenile Death Penalty Today: Present Death Row Inmates Under Juvenile Death Sentences and Death Sentences and Executions for Juvenile Crimes, January 1, 1973, to May 1, 1991.* Cleveland, Ohio: Cleveland-Marshall College of Law, 1991.

Sutherland, Stuart. *The International Dictionary of Psychology.* New York: Continuum, 1988.

Tarrance Group and Greenberg-Lake Staff. *Death Penalty Poll.* Washington, D.C.: The Death Penalty Information Center, 1993.

Taylor, Stuart. "Small Errors Do Not Require Reversal in Death Sentences." *New York Times,* June 1, 1988, p. A26.

Terry, Don, "New Witness Comes Forward Saying Journalist Is Not Killer." *New York Times,* Aug. 11, 1995, p. A14.

Three Centuries of Debate on the Death Penalty. Ed. Greenhaven Staff. St. Paul, Minn.: Greenhaven Press, 1986.

Uniform Crime Reports for the United States 1994. Washington, D.C.: Federal Bureau of Investigation, 1995.

U.S. Catholic Conference. *U.S. Catholic Bishops' Statement on Capital Punishment.* Washington, D.C.: Committee on Social Development and World Peace, 1980. On-line: http://www2.pbs.org/wgbh/pages/frontline/angel/procon/bishopstate.html

U.S. Department of Labor. *Monthly Labor Review* 119/5 (May 1996).

Urban Research Institute, University of Louisville. *Attitudes in the State of Kentucky on the Death Penalty.* New York: Amnesty International, 1989.

Van Braght, Thieleman J. *The Bloody Theater or Martyrs Mirror of the Defenseless Christians.* Dutch original, 1660. English trans., Scottdale, Pa.: Herald Press, 1938 plus reprints.

Von Drehle, Dave. *Amongst the Lowest of the Dead: The Culture of Death Row.* New York: Times Books, Random House, 1995.

——————. "Price Tag Changed Minds in Kansas." *Miami Herald.* n.d.

Weaver, Nolene B. *Offenders in Idaho's Developmental Disabilities and Criminal Justice System.* Boise, Idaho: Idaho State Council on Developmental Disabilities, 1988.

Weissbrodt, David. "New Poll Shows Minnesotans Strongly Prefer Life Sentence over Death Penalty." Report on a poll conducted by the University of Minnesota Center for Survey Research, Oct.-Dec., 1992.

Wesely, Scott. "As Otey Executed, 'All Our Souls Are Diminished.' " *Nebraskans Against the Death Penalty Newsletter.* Sept. 1994, p. 1.

The World Almanac and Book of Facts 1993. New York: World Almanac, 1992.

Wormser, Rene A. *The Story of the Law and the Men Who Made It from Earliest Times to the Present.* New York: Simon and Schuster, 1962.

Yoder, John Howard. *The Christian and Capital Punishment.* Institute of Mennonite Studies Pamphlet Series, no. 1, Newton, Kan.: Faith & Life Press, 1961.

Yoder, John Howard, and H. Wayne House. *Capital Punishment, Two Views.* Dallas: Word Books, 1991.

Zehr, Howard. *Changing Lenses: A New Focus for Crime and Justice.* Scottdale, Pa.: Herald Press, 1990.

——————. *Death as a Penalty.* Elkhart, Ind.: MCC U.S. Office of Criminal Justice, 1987.
——————. *Doing Life: Reflections of Men and Women Serving Life Sentences.* Portraits and Interviews. Intercourse, Pa.: Good Books, 1996.

——————. "MCC Commentary: Executing the Innocent—U.S. v. Biblical Justice." *Lifelines,* no. 59 (Jan.-Mar. 1993).

Index

The Author

Gardner C. Hanks was born in Chicago in 1947. He was brought up in Michigan and has lived in Illinois, Wyoming, New York, Florida, Iowa, Minnesota, and currently in Boise, Idaho.

He has master's degrees in library science from the State University of New York in Albany and in adult education from Florida State University. He has had much experience working in numerous libraries and is presently a professional librarian at Idaho State Library. He is also an adult educator.

Hanks is the Idaho State Death Penalty Action Coordinator for Amnesty International. He has served as spiritual adviser for death row inmates in Idaho.

Hanks is married to Martha Sue Hanks. They have two daughters, Karin (1977) and Kathryn (1985). He is a member of Hyde Park Mennonite Fellowship, where he recently served as elder.